APPROVED WORKBOOK

Chartered Institute for Securities & Investment

Level 3

Certificate in Investment Administration™

Unit 2 – FSA Financial Regulation

Practice and Revision Kit

user 4QSR =BPP
6DF 94649

Syllabus version 16

Contents

ISBN 978 07517 8228 8

© BPP Learning Media Ltd – December 2010

£35.00

Question Bank

Contents

1. The Regulatory Environment

Questions

1. **Which of the following is true of the Financial Services Authority (FSA)?**

    A   It is funded by the Treasury

    B   Its staff are Crown agents

    C   Its Board members are appointed by the Chancellor of the Exchequer

    D   Its governing body is made up solely of the users of investment services

2. **All of the following are Recognised Investment Exchanges (RIEs), except**

    A   London Stock Exchange

    B   LIFFE Administration and Management

    C   New York Stock Exchange

    D   London Metal Exchange

3. **Responsibilities relating to financial stability have been divided between the Bank of England, HM Treasury and the FSA by**

    A   A Memorandum of Understanding

    B   The implementation of the Turner Review

    C   An emergency Statutory Instrument

    D   The FSA's Business Plan

4. **Individuals undertaking any of the controlled functions are known as**

    A   Appointed representatives

    B   Independent Financial Advisers

    C   Approved persons

    D   Authorised persons

5. **The Tax and Chancery Chamber of the Upper Tribunal is governed by**

    A   A group of financial practitioners

    B   HM Treasury

    C   Financial Services Authority

    D   Ministry of Justice

6. **What is the maximum number of employees permitted to work in an authorised firm's compliance department?**

    A   10

    B   20

    C   50

    D   No maximum

7. **Who regulates the banking system in the UK?**

    A   Bank of England

    B   HM Treasury

    C   Financial Services Authority

    D   Basel Committee on Banking Supervision

8. **Which of the following is contained in the FSA Handbook?**

    A   Decision Procedure and Penalties Manual

    B   Complaints: Approved Persons

    C   Regulation of Professionals

    D   Principles for Approved Firms

9. **The Financial Services Authority is funded by contributions from**

    A   HM Treasury

    B   The Bank of England

    C   The London Stock Exchange

    D   Authorised firms

10. **Which of the following is false regarding Recognised Investment Exchanges?**

    A   Membership confers authorisation to do regulated activities

    B   Membership provides access to a market place in which buyers and sellers may trade

    C   They are recognised by the FSA

    D   They regulate the conduct of participants towards each other via their own exchange rules

11. **Which of the following statements concerning general guidance issued by the FSA is false?**

    A   Non-compliance constitutes a breach of rules

    B   It defines the FSA's perception of best practice

    C   It enables firms to seek clarification reducing the likelihood of a subsequent breach

    D   It details and explains the application of rules

12. **Which of the following statements regarding the FSA is false?**

    A   It must have a system to ensure persons are complying with their obligations when conducting investment business

    B   Its rules are enforceable at law

    C   It authorises people to conduct regulated activities

    D   Someone who is an approved person must follow all of its Statements of Principle

13. **Which of the following is not a Recognised Investment Exchange?**

    A   Plus Markets plc

    B   London Metal Exchange

    C   EDX London

    D   Euroclear UK & Ireland

14. **To whom would an investment exchange apply in order to get recognised status?**

    A   Financial Services Authority

    B   HM Treasury

    C   Department for Business, Innovation & Skills

    D   European Commission

15. **Which of the following is not a Principle for Businesses?**

    A   Integrity

    B   Customers: relationships of trust

    C   Relations with regulators

    D   Customers' assets

16. **SYSC rules on apportionment relate to, and expand on, the Principle for Businesses of**

    A   Integrity

    B   Skill, care and diligence

    C   Management and control

    D   Communication with clients

17. **In respect of Individual Savings Accounts (ISAs), HMRC has a role of**

    A   Issuing guidance on ISAs

    B   Maintaining a register of taxpayers' ISAs

    C   Making regulations governing ISAs

    D   Authorising new ISAs

18. **The FSA characterises its planned approach to supervision as an**

   A 'Inspections based' approach

   B 'Bank examiner' approach

   C 'Outcomes focused' approach

   D 'Compliance focused' approach

19. **An exchange that does not conduct regulated activities or allow electronic access from the UK is known as a**

   A Regulated Investment Exchange

   B Recognised Overseas Investment Exchange

   C Designated Investment Exchange

   D Designated Professional Body

20. **Considering the FSA's approach to Principles Based Regulation, which of the following is not an impact of the Senior Management Arrangements, Systems and Controls sourcebook?**

   A Encourages senior management to take responsibility for the firm's arrangements on matters of interest to the FSA

   B Requires a firm to vest responsibility for an effective and responsible organisation in specific directors and senior managers

   C Creates a common platform of organisational systems and controls

   D Requires a firm to organise and control its affairs using adequate risk management systems

21. **Bearing in mind the Statements of Principles and Code of Practice for Approved Persons, which of the following actions by an approved person would be a breach of Principle for Businesses 1: Integrity?**

   A Misleading a client about the risk of an investment

   B Taking an inordinate amount of time to respond to a request for information from the FSA

   C Failing to explain fully the risk of an investment

   D Failing to disclose a conflict of interest to a client

22. **Which of the following is true regarding the FSA's Principles for Business?**

   A A firm will automatically be disciplined for breach of a principle

   B In order to discipline a firm for breach of a principle, it is the responsibility of the FSA to establish that a principle breach has occurred

   C Customers can claim for breach of a principle

   D Principles apply to all authorised firms equally irrespective of their type of business

23. **You are an employee of an authorised firm. To whom would the Chartered Institute for Securities Investment (CISI) advise that you should not take a concern?**

    A Line manager

    B CISI

    C CEO

    D Non-Executive Director

24. **MiFID imposes a general requirement that transaction records for MiFID business must be kept**

    A For five years

    B For six years

    C For seven years

    D For ten years

25. **A distinguishing feature of a so-called 'dark pool' operated by a Multilateral Trading Facility (MTF) is that it**

    A Enables international transactions to be executed without regulatory oversight

    B Does not post prices publicly before trades are made

    C Avoids disclosure requirements where clients' holdings cross 3% and subsequent thresholds

    D Allows order allocation priority to be given to specific clients

26. **Which one of the following types of provision in the FSA Handbook is not binding?**

    A Statements of Principle for Approved Persons

    B Directions

    C Guidance

    D Rules

27. **Industry Guidance:**

    A Includes Codes of Practice and similar Statements generated by trade associations and professional bodies

    B Includes directions and requirements given under various powers conferred by FSMA 2000 and relevant statutory instruments

    C Must be followed fully in order to comply fully with FSA requirements

    D Is mandatory if it is FSA-confirmed

Answers

1.   **C**   The FSA is funded by levies on authorised firms. Its employees are not Crown agencies/civil servants as it is not a government department. The FSA's governing body should contain a balance between users and practitioners

           See Section 1.5 of your Study Text

2.   **C**   The New York Stock Exchange is a DIE

           See Sections 7.4 and 7.5 of your Study Text

3.   **A**   The Memorandum of Understanding (MOU) on financial stability was revised in 2006 and seeks to address the issue of maintaining confidence and stability in the financial system. The MOU divides responsibility between the 'Tripartite Authorities' – the Bank of England, HM Treasury and the FSA

           See Section 1.6 of your Study Text

4.   **C**   'Authorised persons' refers to firms, not individuals

           See Section 3.1 of your Study Text

5.   **D**   TCCUT is independent of the FSA

           See Section 7.10 of your Study Text

6.   **D**   There is no maximum

           See Section 5.2 of your Study Text

7.   **C**   This power passed to the FSA as part of the Bank of England Act 1998

           See Section 1.1.2 of your Study Text

8.   **A**   There are no Sourcebook called Complaints: Approved Persons; Regulation of Professionals; or Principles for Approved Firms

           See Section 8.3 of your Study Text

9.   **D**   Authorised firms pay levies to the FSA

           See Section 1.5 of your Study Text

10.   **A**   An RIE is exempt from authorisation. It is also important to note that members of an RIE, e.g. investment banks, are not exempt

           See Section 7.4 of your Study Text

11.   **A**   Guidance notes are simply there to provide advice; they are not rules and a firm cannot be disciplined for a breach

           See Section 8.5 of your Study Text

12.   **D**   Only the **first four** Statements of Principle apply to all approved persons. The final three principles only apply to those doing a significant influence function

           See Section 3.4 of your Study Text

13. **D** Euroclear UK & Ireland is a Recognised Clearing House (RCH)

See Section 7.4 and 7.6 of your Study Text

14. **A** The FSA grants recognition. Once recognised, the exchange is exempt from S19 FSMA 2000 – the general prohibition

See Section 1.4 of your Study Text

15. **D** **Clients' assets** is the correct Principle

See Section 2.3 of your Study Text

16. **C** SYSC states a firm must take **reasonable care** to establish and maintain appropriate systems and controls

See Section 5.1 of your Study Text

17. **A** HM Revenue & Customs issues guidance on ISAs, which are governed by Treasury Regulations

See Section 7.11 of your Study Text

18. **C** The FSA's Chief Executive Hector Sants has characterised the focus of the Authority's philosophy as resting not *per se* on principles, but rather on judging the consequences of the actions of the firms and the individuals supervised: this is what is meant by outcomes-focused regulation

See Sections 2.6 and 6.2 of your Study Text

19. **C** Examples of Designated Investment Exchanges include the NYSE and the TSE

See Section 7.7 of your Study Text

20. **B** SYSC encourages firms to vest responsibility but does not require this

See Section 5 of your Study Text

21. **A** The key word here is 'misleading', since this implies that the approved person is acting wilfully. The other examples might just be a result of incompetence, which could be a breach of Principle 2: Skill, Care and Diligence

See Sections 3.2 to 3.4 of your Study Text

22. **B** It would be unreasonable for the FSA to discipline without having sufficient evidence

See Section 2 of your Study Text

23. **C** You can use the mnemonic 'SNAIL' (SII (now the CISI), Non-executive directors, audit committee, internal compliance, line manager). The CEO is not included in this list

See Section 4 of your Study Text

24. **A** The five-year rule does not apply to non-MiFID business which may be subject to other requirements but should generally be kept for as long as is relevant for their purpose

See Section 5.2 of your Study Text

25. **B**   Examples of such MTFs include Turquoise, Chi-X and BATS Europe

See Section 7.8 of your Study Text

26. **C**   Guidance ('G') is not binding. Directions ('D') are given under various powers conferred by FSMA 2000 and relevant statutory instruments, and are binding on the persons or categories of person to whom they are addressed

See Section 8.5 of your Study Text

27. **A**   Industry Guidance help members of trade and professional bodies to understand and follow good practice in meeting regulatory requirements. The FSA will not take action against a person for behaviour that it considers to be in line with guidance. Industry Guidance is not mandatory and is one way, but not the only way, to comply with requirements. The FSA does not presume that because firms are not complying with it they are not meeting FSA requirements

See Section 8.6 of your Study Text

2. The Financial Services and Markets Act 2000

Questions

1. **Which of the following are investments under FSMA 2000?**

    I American Depositary Receipts
    II Certificates of Deposit
    III Premium Bonds
    IV Bank loans

    A I, II, III and IV
    B I, II and IV
    C I and II
    D II and III

2. **Which of the following would not be regarded as carrying on investment business under FSMA?**

    A Arranging deals in investments
    B Advising on investments in a *Financial Times* column
    C Publishing a tip sheet
    D Giving advice on investments as a trustee

3. **All of the following are investments, except**

    A Bulldog bonds
    B Certificates of deposit
    C Unit trusts investing in tangible property
    D Futures entered into for commercial purposes

4. **What is the maximum penalty in a Magistrates' Court for conducting unauthorised investment business?**

    A Six months' imprisonment or a fine of £5,000
    B Six months' imprisonment and a fine of £5,000
    C Six months' imprisonment or an unlimited fine
    D Six months' imprisonment and an unlimited fine

5. **Which of the following may prompt the FSA to question an individual's fitness and propriety for approval purposes?**

   I   Their being refused membership to another financial organisation

   II   The discovery of their provision of inaccurate information to their employer

   III A previous conviction

   IV The repossession of their property

   A I, II, III and IV

   B I, II and III

   C I and II

   D II and IV

6. **What notice is required for an FSA surveillance team to enter an authorised firm's premises?**

   A None

   B Reasonable notice

   C One week

   D One day

7. **All of the following are controlled functions, except the function of**

   A Compliance oversight

   B Significant management function

   C Money Laundering Reporting Officer

   D Investment adviser

8. **Which of the following would not be covered under the 'Governing Function' category of controlled functions?**

   A Chief Executive

   B Director

   C Apportionment and oversight

   D Non-executive director

9. **Which of the following would be exempt from authorisation with respect to taking deposits only?**

   A Student Loans Company

   B English Tourist Board

   C LIFFE

   D Bank of England

10. **Which of the following is not a threshold condition for becoming authorised?**

A Custody of investments

B Registered office and head office in the same country

C Adequate resources

D Legal status

11. **A firm must inform the FSA that an approved person has stopped performing a controlled function within**

A Five calendar days

B Seven calendar days

C Seven business days

D Fourteen business days

12. **Which of the following is not relevant when assessing an individual's fitness and propriety?**

A Competence and capability

B Integrity

C Financial soundness

D Age

13. **What is the maximum amount the FSA can fine an approved person?**

A An unlimited amount

B £100,000,000

C £500,000

D £5,000

14. **The FSA defines a 'controller' of an authorised firm as which two of the following?**

I   A person holding 10% or more of the shares in the firm
II   A person who is able to exercise significant influence over the management of the firm
III A person holding 15% or more of the shares in the firm
IV   A person holding 20% or more of the shares in the firm

A I and IV

B I and II

C II and III

D II and IV

15. **Which of the following best describes the Regulatory Decisions Committee (RDC)?**

A A committee of the Financial Ombudsman Service

B A body appointed by HM Treasury comprising practitioners and individuals

C Responsible for assessing appeals against the Financial Services Compensation Scheme

D Responsible for taking disciplinary action against authorised/approved persons

16. **In order for a person to prove fitness and propriety to get FSA approval, they must show**

   A   Financial integrity, competence, good reputation, integrity and honesty

   B   Competence

   C   Good reputation, integrity and honesty

   D   Integrity, honesty and good reputation

17. **Who would normally prosecute a firm for conducting unauthorised regulated activities?**

   A   Department for Business, Innovation & Skills

   B   London Stock Exchange

   C   Financial Services Authority

   D   HM Treasury

18. **Which of the following is not a specified investment?**

   A   An endowment policy

   B   A bank deposit with one month's notice

   C   An option on Brent crude oil

   D   A repo

19. **Which of the following types of approach might the FSA use to supervise a firm?**

   A   Diagnostic, monitoring, preventative, remedial

   B   Investigative, supervisory, protective, curative

   C   Diagnostic, supervisory, preventative, curative

   D   Investigative, monitoring, preventative, remedial

20. **If an adviser carries out unauthorised regulated activities, what are the civil consequences?**

   A   The contract is void

   B   The contract is void from the date of prosecution of the adviser

   C   The contract is voidable at the discretion of a court

   D   The contract is voidable at the option of the client

21. **Which of the following would not be a significant influence function?**

   A   Partner

   B   Money Laundering Reporting Officer

   C   Actuarial function

   D   Customer function

22. **Which of the following is not an exempt person under the Regulated Activities Order (as amended)?**

   A London Stock Exchange

   B Lloyd's

   C Appointed representative

   D Member of a designated professional body

23. **Which of the following is not a specified investment?**

   A Shares in an overseas company

   B Sterling-denominated corporate debt

   C National Savings & Investments Savings Certificates

   D Tax-exempt deposit accounts

24. **Which of the following is not a regulated activity?**

   A Arranging currency transactions in Indian rupees

   B Managing a series of Collective Investment Schemes

   C Advising on UK share investments

   D Dealing in overseas government debt

25. **Under s56, what is the maximum penalty in the instance of an unapproved person breaching a prohibition?**

   A Withdrawal of authorisation

   B An unlimited fine

   C A maximum fine of £5,000

   D A civil prosecution

26. **Which of the following is true regarding Decision Notices?**

   A They can be oral or in writing

   B They set out what sanction has been agreed between the Regulatory Decisions Committee and the firm

   C They are served on firms only

   D They are in writing

27. **All of the following are true regarding whistleblowing procedures, except**

   A A firm can exclude the employees' whistleblowing rights in their contract of employment

   B Rules and guidance are set out in SYSC

   C The rules relate to the Public Interest Disclosure Act 1998

   D Whistleblowing would cover making disclosures relating to criminal offences or damage to the environment

28. Who would be excluded from the need to be authorised?

A   A journalist offering advice in a newspaper

B   A broker dealer sending out a circular

C   A party winding up a collective investment scheme

D   A fund manager dealing only for professional clients

29. When will the RDC be required to send a Statutory Notice?

A   When a fine is being imposed

B   When an Investigation Notice is to be issued

C   When the FSA requires a business plan from a company

D   When a firm is requesting additions to its Part IV permissions

30. Who can impose the prohibition on an individual to work in the financial services industry under FSMA 2000?

A   Financial Services Authority

B   Courts

C   Financial Ombudsman Service

D   Upper Tribunal (Tax and Chancery Chamber)

31. Which of the following is part of the FSA?

A   Financial Services Compensation Scheme

B   Financial Ombudsman Service

C   Regulatory Decisions Committee

D   Upper Tribunal (Tax and Chancery Chamber)

32. Which of the following civil remedies is not available to a client with whom a business has conducted unauthorised regulated activities?

A   The ability to avoid the contract

B   The ability to enforce the contract

C   The ability to obtain damages for any loss suffered

D   The ability to prosecute the business in question

33. Which of the following is not a Statutory Notice?

A   Warning Notice

B   Decision Notice

C   Supervisory Notice

D   Determination Notice

34. **What is the criminal penalty for a breach of a Prohibition Order?**

A   A level three fine

B   A prison sentence not exceeding five years

C   A level five fine

D   Five years' imprisonment and a level three fine

35. **Who issues statutory notices for decisions such as fining an investment bank for a breach of FSA rules?**

A   Financial Ombudsman

B   Regulatory Decisions Committee

C   Her Majesty's Treasury

D   Ministry of Justice

36. **Which of the following are specified investments?**

I   Warrants

II   Residential property

III Building Society Deposit Accounts

IV   Commercial Property

A   I and III

B   I, III and IV

C   II, III, and IV

D   II and IV

37. **Which of the following notices would be issued by the RDC when disciplining a firm whilst not going through the full disciplinary process?**

A   Warning Notice

B   Notice of Termination

C   Supervisory Notice

D   Decision Notice

38. **What is the maximum enforceable penalty for a firm which carries on a regulated activity by way of business without being authorised or exempt?**

A   Unlimited fines

B   Six months in jail and a £5,000 fine

C   Two years in jail

D   Two years in jail and an unlimited fine

39. To which committee would a decision to refuse authorisation be referred?

A   The Financial Ombudsman Service

B   The Authorisation Committee

C   The Regulatory Decisions Committee

D   FSA Management Board

40. For which of the following is there an appropriate examination requirement?

A   Advising on regulated mortgage contracts

B   Eligible counterparty business

C   Arranging term life assurance

D   Giving basic advice on stakeholder products

41. Following an issuance of a Decision Notice the RDC decides not to take disciplinary action against the firm. Instead, they replace it with a remedial action. Which of the following notices will be issued?

A   Supervisory

B   Response

C   Warning

D   Discontinuance

42. Which one of the following activities is excluded from authorisation requirement?

A   Dealing with clients on own account

B   Advising on investments

C   Arranging deals in regulated mortgages

D   Writing an article containing investment advice for a magazine

43. Under s71 of FSMA, who can sue for damages?

A   Professional clients

B   Eligible counterparties

C   Private persons

D   Experts

44. Breaches of which of the following are actionable under s150 of FSMA 2000?

A   The Principles for Businesses of the FSA

B   The rules of the FSA

C   The Statements of Principle of the FSA

D   The Guidance Notes of the FSA

45. **Misleading statements are an offence under the**

   A Company Securities (Insider Dealing) Act

   B Companies Acts

   C Criminal Justice Act

   D Financial Services and Markets Act

---

46. **Which of the following statements is true in relation to s397 FSMA 2000?**

   A It is a civil offence which carries a maximum penalty of an unlimited fine

   B It only covers individuals

   C It is an offence to mislead the market either through a statement, promise or forecast

   D It is an offence to use unpublished price sensitive information

---

47. **The provisions to prevent misleading statement and practices set out in s397 of FSMA 2000 relate to which of the following?**

   A Specified investments

   B Regulated investments

   C Recognised investments

   D Relevant investments

Answers

1. **C**   Premium Bonds are exempt as they are products of the UK Government agency, National Savings & Investments. Loans are only regulated as investments when they are mortgages. A CD is a Certificate of Deposit

    See Section 4.4 of your Study Text

2. **B**   The primary purpose of the *Financial Times* is not that of giving investment advice. A trustee is only exempt if not being paid for his services

    See Sections 4.1 and 4.3 of your Study Text

3. **D**   Only futures for **investment purposes** and exchange-traded futures are investments

    See Section 4.4 of your Study Text

4. **B**   The maximum is the worst case where both imprisonment and a fine are imposed

    See Section 1.2 of your Study Text

5. **A**   The FSA may question all of these matters

    See Section 4.10 of your Study Text

6. **A**   Notice is usually given but is not required

    See Section 3 of your Study Text

7. **D**   This is not a specific controlled function

    See Section 4.12 of your Study Text

8. **C**   Apportionment and oversight is not a governing function, but part of the 'required functions' group of controlled functions

    See Section 4.12 of your Study Text

9. **A**   The Student Loans Company has an exemption for deposit taking

    See Section 1.7 of your Study Text

10. **A**   Custody is covered by the regulated activity of safeguarding and administration of investments but is **not** a threshold condition

    See Section 4.7 of your Study Text

11. **C**   Business days, not calendar days!

    See Section 4.11 of your Study Text

12. **D**   Age is not considered to be a relevant factor

    See Section 4.10 of your Study Text

13. **A**   As well as private and public censure and temporary or permanent suspension of approval, the FSA can impose an unlimited fine

    See Section 2.1 of your Study Text

14. **D** This is the precise definition

   See Section 4.8 of your Study Text

15. **D** The RDC is not related to the FOS or the FSCS. It is a body appointed by the FSA, not HM Treasury

   See Section 2.1 of your Study Text

16. **A** These are all factors the FSA will consider

   See Section 4.10 of your Study Text

17. **C** The FSA will prosecute for breaches of s19 FSMA

   See Section 1.1 of your Study Text

18. **C** An option on the Brent crude future would have been a specified investment

   See Section 4.4 of your Study Text

19. **A** These are the specific terms used by the FSA

   See Section 4.9 of your Study Text

20. **D** Voidable is the technical term used

   See Section 1.3 of your Study Text

21. **D** The other three options would certainly be classified as significant influence functions

   See Section 4.12 of your Study Text

22. **B** Members of Lloyd's are exempt persons, but the institution of Lloyd's is not exempt and thus requires authorisation from the FSA

   See Section 1.7 of your Study Text

23. **C** National Savings & Investments products are not specified investments under FSMA 2000. The fact that the deposit account is tax exempt is irrelevant to its status as a specified investment

   See Section 4.4 of your Study Text

24. **A** Arranging deals in investments would have been a regulated activity, however, forex trades are not specified investments

   See Section 4.1 of your Study Text

25. **C** An unapproved person breaching a prohibition order is subject to a maximum fine of £5,000

   See Section 2.7 of your Study Text

26. **D** Decisions Notices must be in writing. The Decision Notice sets out the proposed sanction. This sanction can either be accepted or challenged by the firm. Such a notice may be sent to firms or individuals

   See Sections 2.1 of your Study Text

27.   A   A firm **cannot** exclude employee's rights to blow the whistle on various activities

See Section 4.18 of your Study Text

28.   A   The media/journalists offering advice in a newspaper is an example of an excluded activity (media tip sheets). Those only carrying out excluded activities do not need to seek authorisation under s19 FSMA 2000

See Section 4.3 of your Study Text

29.   A   The RDC will issue a statutory notice generally where the matters involve serious wrongdoing, eg refusing, limiting or narrowing Part IV permission or approved person status, making a prohibition order, imposing fines or issuing public statements of misconduct or restitution orders

See Section 2.1 of your Study Text

30.   A   Section 56 Prohibition Orders are issued by the FSA

See Section 2.7 of your Study Text

31.   C   The Regulatory Decisions Committee is a separate committee of the FSA

See Section 2.1 of your Study Text

32.   D   Prosecution occurs in a criminal case and is not a civil remedy. The other options given are courses of action in the civil court

See Sections 1.1 and 1.3 of your Study Text

33.   D   A Determination Notice is **not** one of the statutory notices that the FSA/RDC can issue

See Sections 2.3 and 2.4 of your Study Text

34.   C   A level five fine is the legal term for the maximum fine of £5,000 in a Magistrates' Court

See Section 2.7 of your Study Text

35.   B   It is the RDC that issues statutory notices

See Section 2.3 of your Study Text

36.   A   We know that commercial property is not a specified investment, so this is the best answer available

See Section 4.4 of your Study Text

37.   A   A Warning Notice is the first notice that the RDC would issue. This could be followed by a Notice of Discontinuation

See Sections 2.3 and 2.4 of your Study Text

38.   D   Be careful: if the question asked about the maximum custodial sentence this would be two years

See Section 1.2 of your Study Text

39.   C   It is the RDC to whom a decision to refuse will be referred

See Section 4.8 of your Study Text

40. **A** The TC sourcebook applies only to business involving retail clients, customers or consumers and no longer applies to wholesale business. Protection-only life insurance and giving advice on stakeholder products are exceptions to the appropriate examination requirement

See Section 4.13 of your Study Text

41. **A** A Supervisory Notice contains requirements from the FSA that would have to be immediately implemented by the authorised firm

See Section 2.1 and 2.3 of your Study Text

42. **D** Example of the excluded activity "Media tip sheets"

See Section 4.3 of your Study Text

43. **C** Remember that a private person and a retail client are not the same thing

See Section 2.8 of your Study Text

44. **B** Only rules are actionable under s150

See Section 2.8 of your Study Text

45. **D** It is covered by s397 of FSMA 2000

See Section 5 of your Study Text

46. **C** Misleading Statements and Practices – s397 is a criminal offence. It is the insider dealing offence that concerns the use of unpublished information and applies only to individuals

See Section 5 of your Study Text

47. **D** The exact term in s397 is 'relevant investments'

See Section 5 of your Study Text

3. Associated Legislation and Regulation

Questions

1. **Which of the following is responsible for insider dealing legislation?**

    A   Financial Services Authority

    B   Department of Business, Innovation & Skills

    C   HM Treasury

    D   London Stock Exchange

2. **Which of the following is false under the 2007 Money Laundering Regulations for an employee of an authorised firm?**

    A   He must arrest the suspect

    B   He must identify the source of the funds

    C   He must report suspicions to his MLRO

    D   He may be required to check the identity of customers

3. **Which of the following is not a principle of the Data Protection Act 1998?**

    A   Personal data shall be processed fairly and lawfully

    B   Personal data shall be adequate, relevant and not excessive

    C   Personal data shall be accurate

    D   Personal data may be kept indefinitely

4. **To have abused a market**

    A   There must be intention but not necessarily effect

    B   There must be intention and effect

    C   There must be effect but not necessarily intention

    D   There need not be effect nor intention

5. **Which of the following statements about insider dealing is false?**

    A   It only relates to unpublished, price-sensitive information

    B   Legislation covers unit trusts

    C   It is prosecuted by the FSA

    D   It cannot be prosecuted if information is passed on in the proper course of duties

6. **Which of the following is not true, in the context of contrasting market abuse with insider dealing?**

    A   Guilt for market abuse is based on the balance of probabilities rather than beyond reasonable doubt

    B   It should be more difficult for the FSA to prove guilt for market abuse

    C   It should be less difficult to impose a fine for market abuse

    D   Market abuse covers commodity derivatives whereas insider dealing does not

7. **A market maker acting in good faith will not be prosecuted for insider dealing because there is a**

    A   Special defence for market makers

    B   General defence

    C   Defence covering bid facilitation

    D   Defence covering stabilisation

8. **Which of the following terms best describes a regular market user?**

    I   Hypothetical person

    II   Reasonable person

    III   Trades on a regular basis

    IV   Used to judge abuse of a market

    A   I and IV

    B   II and III

    C   II, III and IV

    D   I, II, III and IV

9. **Which of the following would not constitute the proceeds of criminal activity for money laundering purposes?**

    A   Tax avoidance

    B   Tax evasion

    C   Funds arising from forgery

    D   Funds from drug trafficking

10. **To verify that client investment funds are legitimate, a firm should do all of the following, except**

    A   Check the client's identity

    B   Check the client's background

    C   Check police records

    D   Check with the MLRO

11. **Assuming that there is no suspicion of money laundering or terrorist financing, a business will normally be able to apply simplified due diligence with respect to anti money laundering checks when the customer is**

    A   A Member of a non-UK Parliament

    B   A Spanish bank

    C   Not physically present

    D   Not resident in the UK

12. **What aspect of behaviour constitutes a potential abuse of the market?**

    A   The behaviour itself

    B   The intent of the behaviour

    C   The motivation of the behaviour

    D   The effect of the behaviour

13. **Inside information could be supplied by which of the following?**

        I   A director

        II   An office cleaner

        III   A secretary

        IV   A shareholder

    A   I or III

    B   I, II or III

    C   I, II, III or IV

    D   II or IV

14. **How will the FSA respond to historic behaviour which would now be considered an abuse of the market where the original behaviour seemed reasonable?**

    A   Tailor their response to the qualifying investment concerned

    B   Decide on the basis of the circumstances at the time

    C   Apply the full and specific letter of the law

    D   Apply current levels of acceptable behaviour

15. **Money Laundering Regulations normally require an ID procedure for which of the following?**

    A   A transaction with a UK authorised bank

    B   A potential new retail client who is resident in the UK

    C   An occasional transaction with a firm bound by the money laundering regulations

    D   An occasional transaction of €12,000

16. **Which of the following is not normally recognised as a typical stage in the money laundering process?**

    A   The placement of cash into the financial system by opening a bank account

    B   Conducting a complex series of financial transactions to confuse the audit trail

    C   Undertaking illegal activities to generate funds to be laundered

    D   Purchasing income generating financial assets with previously invested illegal funds

---

17. **Which of the following statements regarding insider dealing is false?**

    A   Inside information from a primary source is covered

    B   Inside information from a secondary source is covered

    C   Trading must occur for an offence to be committed

    D   Trading need not occur for an offence to be committed

---

18. **Which of the following could be regarded as a suspicious transaction for money laundering purposes?**

    I   A private customer making a one-off £10m purchase of securities

    II   Transferring payments from or into accounts not in the name of the customer

    III   Use by a customer of a credit card in a different name

    IV   A series of unusual payments by a customer totalling less than €15,000 which appear unusual, given the account history

    A   I, II, III and IV

    B   I, II and III

    C   II and IV

    D   I and III

---

19. **The Money Laundering Regulations 2007 cover**

    I   All credit institutions

    II   All firms covered by FSMA 2000

    III   All financial businesses

    IV   Bureaux de Change

    A   I, II, III and IV

    B   I, II and III

    C   II and IV

    D   I and III

---

20. **Which of the following is the maximum penalty for an institution that fails to implement internal reporting procedures in respect of money laundering?**

    A   Two years' imprisonment or an unlimited fine

    B   Five years' imprisonment and an unlimited fine

    C   Two years' imprisonment and an unlimited fine

    D   Six months' imprisonment and the statutory fine

---

21. **Which two of the following penalties may the FSA impose for breaching the market abuse offence?**

    I   Maximum fine of £5,000

    II   Seven years' imprisonment

    III   Public censure

    IV   Discipline of approved persons

A I and II

B II and III

C II and IV

D III and IV

22. **The Money Laundering Reporting Officer is required to make a report to the senior management of an FSA firm**

A Monthly

B Quarterly

C Every financial year

D Every calendar year

23. **Which of the following is false with regard to the Money Laundering Regulations 2007?**

A Identification is not required for general insurance contracts

B The regulations apply to financial institutions and credit institutions

C Where the client is introduced by an authorised firm, the firm can rely on the introducer for identification

D Identification procedures are not required for institutions listed in the Money Laundering Directive

24. **Which of the following would not be an offence under market abuse provisions?**

A Dealing in UK shares with inside information

B Making a misleading statement to distort a market in UK shares

C Misleading practices in securities trading in the UK

D Making a hostile takeover

25. **In which two of the following circumstances would an authorised firm not be expected to identify its clients for money laundering purposes?**

   I   The person is not from the UK
   II An occasional transaction transacted by another financial services institution in the EU
   III An occasional transaction of €35,000
   IV Where the client is acting through another regulated firm which has given written assurance that they have verified the client's identity

   A I and III
   B II and III
   C I and IV
   D II and IV

26. **All of the following are powers available to the FSA if it has found that a person has engaged in market abuse, except**

   A The FSA may make a public statement that a person has engaged in market abuse
   B The FSA may ask the court to impose a restitution order
   C The FSA may impose a maximum fine of £100,000
   D The FSA may ask the court to impose an injunction

27. **Which of the following is not true of insider dealing legislation contained in the Criminal Justice Act 1993, except**

   A Insider dealing is a criminal offence
   B An insider who discloses inside information (other than in the normal course of business) is committing an offence
   C UK equities, gilts and related derivatives are all covered by the legislation
   D The conduct must fall short of the standard expected by a regular user

28. **Under the Data Protection Act 1998, for how long should a firm keep personal data?**

   A Three years from the end of any customer agreement
   B Five years from the date of the transaction
   C For no longer than is necessary for the firm's purposes
   D Indefinitely

29. **Firm XYZ takes a risk-based approach to AML procedures. This is because**

   A A risk-based approach is mandatory under MLR 2007
   B The firm has clients who are high net worth individuals
   C The firm has clients who are politically exposed persons
   D The role of Money Laundering Reporting Officer is not performed exclusively by one person

30. **Under the UKLA Model Code, if the Chairman wants to deal in the company's shares, permission must be granted by**

    A   The company's Board

    B   The Financial Director

    C   The Chief Executive

    D   Another director

31. **Under the Data Protection Act 1998, personal data should not be transferred outside which one of the following, unless adequate protection of the rights and freedoms of subjects can be guaranteed?**

    A   The UK

    B   The firm

    C   The EEA

    D   The EU

32. **In the context of AML measures, for what reason should Enhanced Due Diligence normally be applied for politically exposed persons (PEPs) from outside the UK?**

    A   Because PEPs are well known and so simplified due diligence can be bypassed

    B   Because the position of PEPs may make them vulnerable to corruption

    C   Because PEPs will not normally be able to verify their identity in the normal way

    D   Because it is vital to keep transactions involving PEPs confidential

33. **What is the maximum penalty for failing to report terrorism?**

    A   Two years' imprisonment and an unlimited fine

    B   Five years' imprisonment and an unlimited fine

    C   Seven years' imprisonment and an unlimited fine

    D   Fourteen years' imprisonment and an unlimited fine

34. **The Proceeds of Crime Act 2002 Section 333A makes tipping off an offence for**

    A   All persons

    B   Approved persons

    C   Persons within the regulated sector

    D   Money Laundering Reporting Officers

35. **To whom should an employee report suspected terrorist offences, according to legislative requirements?**

    ·A   Their manager or the MLRO

    B   A nominated officer or their MLRO

    C   A nominated officer or the police

    D   A nominated officer or their manager

36. **If a director wishes to deal in shares of his own company, from whom should permission be sought?**

    A   The Finance Officer

    B   The CEO

    C   The Chairman

    D   The Human Resources Department

37. **Under insider dealing legislation, who can use a special defence if acting 'in good faith'?**

    A   Market maker

    B   Firm initiating a takeover

    C   Manager of a regulated collective investment scheme

    D   Non-executive company directors

38. **Market abuse is**

    A   Behaviour in relation to qualifying investments on a prescribed market

    B   Behaviour intended to distort the market

    C   Behaviour in relation to specified investments on a prescribed market

    D   Behaviour that breaches Stock Exchange rules

39. **If an employee suspects money laundering activity, within what time period must they report their suspicions to their Money Laundering Reporting Officer (MLRO)?**

    A   Immediately

    B   As soon as is reasonably practicable

    C   Within one business day

    D   Within five business days

40. **Which of the following are true of the Model Code for Directors?**

    I   It is a set of rules that must be followed by all approved persons in positions of significant influence

    II   It specifies how much, and how frequently, directors are allowed to trade in the company's shares

    III   It requires that directors should not trade in the company's shares in the two months before results are announced

    IV   It recommends that the Chairman has responsibility for approving all share dealings by directors

    A   I and IV

    B   II and IV

    C   I and II

    D   III and IV

41. **Which of the following cannot be prosecuted under insider dealing regulations as set out in the Criminal Justice Act 1993?**

   A   An employee

   B   A shareholder

   C   A company

   D   A director

42. **You suspect money laundering at your authorised firm and, after much deliberation, you report your suspicions to the MLRO five months later. What is the maximum sentence you could receive?**

   A   Nothing as you have reported suspicions

   B   Censure but no fine/imprisonment

   C   Five years' imprisonment

   D   Fourteen years' imprisonment

43. **You are an employee of an FSA-authorised firm and you suspect that a customer may be involved in money laundering. Which of the following are true in respect of your duties?**

   A   The Chief Executive has responsibility for reporting suspicions to the Money Laundering Reporting Officer

   B   The Money Laundering Reporting Officer must report suspicions to SOCA

   C   You must report suspicions to the Money Laundering Reporting Officer

   D   You must report all suspicions to SOCA

44. **What is the best description of market abuse?**

   A   A civil offence

   B   A criminal offence

   C   A criminal offence with a civil standard of proof

   D   A breach of contract

45. **With regard to the Money Laundering requirements, which of the following is not true?**

   A   Systems and controls set up to manage money laundering risk should be comprehensive and proportionate to the nature, scale and complexity of the firm

   B   The FSA's Senior Management Arrangements, Systems and Controls (SYSC) rules require training to be given to staff every two years

   C   The JMLSG Guidance Notes have been approved by the Treasury

   D   The director or senior manager given overall responsibility for the establishment and maintenance of a firm's AML/CFT systems and controls can also be the firm's MLRO

46. **Which of the following is true of both the insider dealing and market abuse legislation?**

   A   They both guard against acts designed to mislead the market

   B   They carry identical penalties

   C   They concern information not generally known to the market

   D   They relate to the same investment instruments

47. **According to the Model Code for Directors' Dealings, directors should not undertake trades in the shares of their company**

   A   For two months prior to the announcement of results

   B   For two months prior to the publication of accounts

   C   For two months prior to the publication of results

   D   For two months prior to the end of the reporting period

48. **Where would you (as an individual) look for legislation on money laundering prevention?**

   A   Financial Services and Markets Act 2000

   B   Criminal Justice Act 1993

   C   Proceeds of Crime Act 2002

   D   Money Laundering Regulations

49. **When would a person working in the regulated sector be punished for a breach of s333A POCA 2002?**

   A   When they failed to disclose knowledge of money laundering to their MLRO

   B   When they failed to adequately identity a client

   C   When they knowingly transferred suspicious funds

   D   When they made a prejudiced disclosure that affected an investigation

50. **Which of the following does not contain provisions relating to money laundering?**

   A   Money Laundering Regulations 2007

   B   Proceeds of Crime Act 2002

   C   FSA Senior Management Arrangements, Systems and Controls Sourcebook

   D   Criminal Justice Act 1993

51. **Which of the following is not a legitimate contributing reason for a company delaying the disclosure of inside information?**

   A   The company's viability is in grave imminent danger

   B   The company is in negotiations to ensure its long-term financial recovery

   C   The share price may rise substantially if the information is released

   D   The company is able to ensure that the information will be kept confidential

52. **Behaviour is outside the scope of the legislation on market abuse generally if it occurs**

    A Through electronic access to markets

    B Outside the UK

    C Outside the UK and does not relate to qualifying investments

    D Outside the UK and through electronic access to markets

53. **Who can instigate proceedings for insider dealing according to FSMA 2000?**

    A Financial Ombudsman

    B Financial Services Authority

    C Serious Organised Crime Agency

    D Department of Business, Innovation & Skills

54. **Complying with what will indicate that the money laundering regulations have been met?**

    A JMLSG Guidance

    B Counter-Terrorism Act 2008

    C SOCA Guidance

    D Criminal Justice Act 1993

55. **Which of the following would be considered to be criminal property under the Proceeds of Crime Act?**

    A All property

    B All property of the criminal

    C All benefits obtained by illegal activity

    D Money only

56. **An investor's change in shareholdings in a listed UK company need not be publicised if the change in voting rights is**

    A From 2.1% to 3.8%

    B From 2.9% to 3.7%

    C From 7.1% to 6.9%

    D From 2.8% to 0.9%

57. **Which one of the following statements is true in relation to S397 FSMA 2000?**

    A It is a civil offence which carries a maximum penalty of an unlimited fine

    B It only covers individuals

    C It is an offence to mislead the market either through a statement, promise or forecast

    D It is an offence to use unpublished price sensitive information

58. **The provisions to prevent misleading statements and practices set out in s397 FSMA 2000 relate to**

   A   Specified investments

   B   Regulated investments

   C   Recognised investments

   D   Relevant investments

59. **The purpose of the UKLA's Model Code for Director's Dealings is to**

   A   Protect the directors from suspicions of wrongdoing in using unpublished confidential information for their own personal gain

   B   Prevent directors from purchasing the securities issued by their company

   C   Prevent the company from issuing shares to their directors

   D   Restrict directors' right to sell the shares forcing them to own the securities for at least two years

60. **The FSA has stated that it may NOT prosecute a person for market abuse if**

   A   The person shows that he did not expect to profit

   B   The person shows that all precautions have been taken and all due diligence is in place to avoid market abuse

   C   The person shows that he would have dealt anyway

   D   The person shows that he was in possession of market information

61. **Which one of the following dealings cannot give rise to prosecution for insider dealing?**

   A   Private trades between investors

   B   Dealing through a UK broker on an MTF

   C   Dealing on a UK regulated exchange

   D   Dealing in CFDs on interest rates

62. **In the course of reporting suspicious transactions the employee will not be found guilty of money laundering offences under POCA 2002 if he**

   A   Reports suspicious transactions to his MLRO

   B   Deals for a client previously reported to the MLRO as engaging in suspicious transactions

   C   Discloses to the client in a durable medium that he is subject to investigation

   D   Verifies the client's name and address by inspecting identity documents

63. **In which one of the following ways can terrorist financing typically can differ from money laundering?**

   A   Funds come from a legitimate source

   B   The amount of money involved is unusually large

   C   The transactions follow unusual patterns

   D   The transaction is carried out on behalf of an overseas client

64. **Following a company's listing on an exchange, it will now be subject to UK Disclosure and Transparency rules. One purposes of those rules is**

   A   To prohibit firms from disclosing price sensitive information to the market

   B   To outline cases when issue of price sensitive information to the market can be delayed

   C   To prevent the company from issuing extra shares to the investors

   D   To prevent the company from purchasing securities in other companies

65. **Under Principle 8 of the Data Protection Act, which one of following is a geographical boundary for free distribution of personal data?**

   A   UK

   B   European Union

   C   European Economic Area

   D   G10 countries

66. **Host state rules will apply to which of the following?**

   A   French investment firm cross-border trading with a UK firm

   B   Branch of an inwardly passported UK firm

   C   American investment firm cross-border trading with a UK firm

   D   Singapore registered bank accepting deposits from UK clients

67. **Which one of the following is not a requirement of the Prospectus Directive?**

   A. Approval of a prospectus by a relevant home state competent authority

   B   Prospectus should contain information identified in the Directive

   C   Issuers will have to follow the same disclosure procedures for every market where they list the securities

   D   Home state listing authority approved prospectus must be accepted for listing purposes throughout the EU

68. **A fund manager buys a large number of ABC shares near the end of the day, aiming to drive the stock price higher to improve the performance of the fund. His actions can be found illegal under**

   A   Criminal Justice Act 1993

   B   Financial Services and Markets Act 2000

   C   Guidance on Market Abuse provided by JMLSG

   D   Serious Organised Crime and Police Act 2005

69. Which of the following will not be considered market abuse as stated in the Code of Market Conduct?

A   Market making

B   Timely disclosure and dissemination of information on listed companies

C   Stockbroker is executing a client's order

D   Applying for authorisation before publishing tip sheets in media

70. Which of the following is the best definition of passporting?

A   An authorised EEA firm passporting its authorisation into a Member State

B   An EU firm passporting its authorisation into a Member State

C   A FATF firm passporting its authorisation into a Member State

D   An EEA firm opening a subsidiary in a Member State, having notified the regulator

71. The main purpose of UCITS is to

A   Avoid repetition when issuing offering proposals in EEA member states

B   Harmonise Conduct of Business rules

C   Enable sale of unit trusts and OEICs in the EU on the basis of home authorisation

D   Create a single market in financial instruments

72. Identify which of the following investments a UCITS scheme can invest in.

    I   Transferable securities
    II   Derivative and forward transactions
    III   Deposits
    IV   Units in other collective investment schemes

A   I and II

B   I, II and III

C   III only

D   I, II, III and IV

73. Which of the following is not a core investment service or activity under MiFID?

A   Execution of orders on behalf of clients

B   Dealing on own account

C   Advising on mergers and acquisitions

D   Placing of financial instruments

74. **How would you best describe 'Basel II'?**

    A An agreement concerning the movement of capital between EU member countries and Switzerland

    B An agreement based on the Basel Capital Accord relating to financial resources requirements

    C An agreement relating to capital requirements that preceded the Capital Adequacy Directive (CAD)

    D An agreement relating to the capital requirements of insurance companies and credit card companies

75. **MiFID applies to investment activities in relation to all of the following financial instruments, except**

    A Commodity derivatives

    B Freight rate derivatives

    C Currencies

    D Money market instruments

76. **All of the following are MiFID investment services and activities, except**

    A Portfolio management

    B Operation of an Multilateral Trading Facility

    C Investment advice

    D Investment research

77. **Which one of the following is a MiFID investment firm?**

    A Employee share scheme

    B Commodity trader

    C Professional investor investing for himself

    D Broker/dealer

78. **The main purpose of MiFID is to**

    A Remove barriers for passporting ancillary services

    B Enlarge responsibilities of home state regulators

    C Harmonise client asset handling procedures

    D Extend a list of passported services and harmonise home rules

79. **What type of fund is not permitted under UCITS III?**

    A Derivatives

    B Gold

    C Money market

    D Warrants

80. **Which of the following businesses' activities are fully within the range of MiFID?**

       I   A stockbroking firm

      II   An insurance company

     III   A collective investment scheme

     IV   A credit institution accepting deposits

A I, II, III and IV

B None of the above

C I, II and III

D II, III and IV

81. **Who would be exempt from the need to seek authorisation?**

A A branch of an US investment bank advising on investments

B A UK investment firm providing financial services to an investor based in France

C A UK investment firm operating a pension scheme for a German company

D A French firm writing an insurance contract for a UK-based client

Answers

1. **C** The legislation is the responsibility of the Treasury. Investigation and prosecution are the responsibility of the LSE and FSA respectively

   See Section 1.1 of your Study Text

2. **A** Money laundering legislation does not require an individual to assist in the arrest of the money launderer

   See Section 3.5 of your Study Text

3. **D** Principle 5 provides that personal data processed for any purpose shall not be kept for longer than is necessary for that purpose. Data should be reviewed regularly to determine whether it can be deleted

   See Section 6.2 of your Study Text

4. **C** It is possible to have abused a market without intention to do so, for example through. Legislation is 'effect-based'

   See Section 2.7 of your Study Text

5. **B** Unit trusts, in which there is no secondary market, are excluded from the legislation

   See Section 1.1 of your Study Text

6. **B** Market abuse is a civil offence requiring a lower burden of proof than the criminal offence of insider dealing. Therein lies the deterrent power of the market abuse legislation; far easier to successfully prosecute and far wider reaching

   See Sections 1.1 and 2.1 of your Study Text

7. **A** But only as long as they are acting in good faith; if not, they may be prosecuted

   See Section 1.5.1 of your Study Text

8. **D** It is the expectations of customers who regularly use the markets, and who understand how they work, that will be used to judge market abuse. Of course, there is no one single regular market user; they only exist in a hypothetical sense

   See Section 2.3 of your Study Text

9. **A** Minimising your tax liability through 'tax avoidance' (as opposed to tax evasion) is not criminal activity

   See Section 3.1 of your Study Text

10. **C** Going to the police should not be necessary at this stage

    See Section 3.5 of your Study Text

11. **B** Credit or financial institutions in the EEA or under equivalent regimes qualify for simplified due diligence

    See Section 3.10 of your Study Text

12. **D** The market abuse legislation is effects-based

    See Section 2.7 of your Study Text

13. **C** All employees are, by virtue of their office, potential holders of inside information. Shareholders are also a potential inside source

    See Section 1.2 of your Study Text

14. **B** The FSA have stated that they will apply their own discretion given the circumstances prevailing at the time of the alleged abuse

    See Section 2 of your Study Text

15. **B** Firms are required to carry out identification procedures on establishing new business unless, for example, it is a transaction with an EEA financial institution or is less than €15,000 in value

    See Section 3.5 of your Study Text

16. **C** The three stages in the money laundering process are placement, layering and integration. The criminal activity to get the funds in the first place is not included

    See Section 3.1 of your Study Text

17. **C** **Disclosing** inside information can be prosecuted even if trading has not occurred

    See Section 1.3 of your Study Text

18. **A** All of these could be suspicious. In IV, the fact that the transactions are less than €15,000 is not relevant

    See Section 3.5 of your Study Text

19. **A** These regulations are generally all-inclusive

    See Section 3.5 of your Study Text

20. **C** The maximum would be a prison sentence together with a fine. Remember, liability does not require money laundering to have happened; simply not having the appropriate procedures in place is deemed to be a failure to implement the correct procedures

    See Section 3.5 of your Study Text

21. **D** The fine is unlimited. As market abuse is a civil offence, there is no jail sentence available. As an FSA rule would have been broken, an approved person could face FSA disciplinary action

    See Section 2.9 of your Study Text

22. **D** Note that this requirement relates to calendar years and not the financial year of the firm involved

    See Section 3.7.1 of your Study Text

23. **A** It is permissible for one FSA firm to rely on written assurance from another FSA firm for money laundering identification purposes

    See Section 3.5 of your Study Text

24.   **D**   A hostile takeover is not in itself abusive

See Section 2.6 of your Study Text

25.   **D**   The location of the client is irrelevant. Occasional transactions of €15,000 or more must be subjected to standard customer due diligence

See Section 3.10 of your Study Text

26.   **C**   The FSA can ask the court to impose an injunction, restitution or other penalty. Fines can be unlimited

See Section 2.9 of your Study Text

27.   **D**   The regular user test is part of the civil offence of **market abuse**, not the criminal offence of insider dealing

See Sections 1.1 and 2.3 of your Study Text

28.   **C**   The requirement to keep records for three or six years or indefinitely is under the FSA's Conduct of Business Rules, whilst the requirement to keep records for five years is under the Money Laundering Regulations

See Section 6.4 of your Study Text

29.   **A**   A risk-based approach is mandatory under the 2007 regulations

See Section 3.8.4 of your Study Text

30.   **C**   If the Chairman wishes to deal, then he must ask permission from the Chief Executive Officer

See Section 5.4 of your Study Text

31.   **C**   This is Principle 8 of the legislation which states that adequate protection must be ensured for the freedom and rights of data subjects, in relation to data processing, if transferring data outside the European Economic Area (EU countries plus Norway, Iceland and Liechtenstein)

See Section 6.2 of your Study Text

32.   **B**   It is PEPs' vulnerability to corruption which leads to the EDD requirement

See Section 3.8.4 of your Study Text

33.   **B**   This is the same as failing to report knowledge of suspicion of money laundering

See Section 4.6 of your Study Text

34.   **C**   Under s333A, a person within the regulated sector commits an **offence** if, based on information they acquire in the course of business that is likely to prejudice any investigation, they disclose that information has been passed to the police, HMRC, a Nominated Officer (generally, the firm's MLRO) or the Serious Organised Crime Agency, or that an investigation into money laundering allegations is being contemplated or carried out

See Section 3.6.3 of your Study Text

35. **C**   A nominated officer of a firm will normally be the MLRO. Although you may report suspected terrorism to your manager, this is not what the Anti-Terrorism, Crime and Security Act 2001 requires

See Section 4.6.1 of your Study Text

36. **C**   This is a requirement under the Model Code for Directors' Dealing of the UKLA. Permission should normally be sought from the Chairman of the company or other designated persons

See Section 5.4 of your Study Text

37. **A**   Market makers acting in good faith, and following the rules of the Stock Exchange, will be able to rely on this special defence

See Section 1.5.1 of your Study Text

38. **A**   While the other answers may have an element of truth, the best description is answer A, which covers the benchmarking exercise to determine if market abuse has been conducted or not

See Section 2.1 of your Study Text

39. **B**   Failing to report suspicions as soon as is reasonably practicable is a criminal offence under legislation

See Section 3.3.2 of your Study Text

40. **D**   It is the Chairman, or any other designated person, who should approve directors' share dealings. The Model Code does not restrict the frequency or size of transactions

See Section 5.4 of your Study Text

41. **C**   'An insider' is defined as 'an individual who has information in his possession that he knows is inside information, and knows is from an 'inside source'. An individual would include a director, employee, or shareholder of an issuer of securities, or a person who has access to the information by virtue of their employment, office or profession. A person will also be an inside source if he receives the information directly, or indirectly, from one of the above and satisfies the general definition above

See Section 1.2 of your Study Text

42. **C**   Reporting must occur as soon as possible. The delay of five months breaches this, so you could still be guilty of failure to report, which carries a five-year penalty

See Section 3.5 of your Study Text

43. **C**   Failure to report to the Money Laundering Reporting Officer (MLRO) carries a maximum penalty in the Crown Court of five years' imprisonment and an unlimited fine. The MLRO must report all suspicions to SOCA. However, the question asks about **your** duties as the employee

See Section 3.6.2 of your Study Text

44. **A** As defined in s118 of FSMA 2000, market abuse is a civil offence, requiring a civil standard of proof – the balance of probabilities – even though it carries what is usually a criminal penalty of an unlimited fine. This should make the offence easier to prosecute than equivalent criminal offences, which require guilt beyond reasonable doubt

See Section 2.1 of your Study Text

45. **B** The SYSC rules require that 'appropriate' training is given to employees; however, no timescales are given

See Section 3.7.1 of your Study Text

46. **C** The market abuse and insider dealing legislation both cover behaviour based on information not generally available. Remember of course that market abuse also covers false or misleading impressions and behaviour that distorts the market (whereas insider dealing does not). Insider dealing covers only a list of specific investments, whereas market abuse covers a wider range of qualifying investments on any prescribed market. Therefore, C is the best answer, as it represents the most obvious area of commonality for the two offences

See Sections 1.1 and 2.1 of your Study Text

47. **A** The rule concerning closed periods applies to the two months prior to the announcement of full or half-year results, which will normally be in the form of an announcement to the Stock Exchange, via a Regulatory Information Service (RIS). For quarterly reporting, this period is reduced to one month

See Section 5.4 of your Study Text

48. **C** The Proceeds of Crime Act 2002 (POCA 2002) contains money laundering legislation applicable to individuals

See Section 3.6 of your Study Text

49. **D** Section 333A of POCA 2002 relates to tipping off/alerting the money launderer that they are under investigation

See Section 3.6.3 of your Study Text

50. **D** The relevant provisions of CJA 1993 were repealed some years ago and replaced by provisions in POCA 2002

See Section 3 of your Study Text

51. **C** The Disclosure and Transparency Rules provide that an issuer may delay the public disclosure of inside information, such as not to prejudice its legitimate interests, provided that the public would not be likely to be misled and the issuer is able to ensure the confidentiality of the information. Public disclosure of information could be delayed for a limited period if the firm's financial viability is in 'grave and imminent danger', to avoid undermining negotiations to ensure the firm's long-term financial recovery

See Section 5.2.3 of your Study Text

52. **C** Behaviour will only constitute market abuse if it occurs in the UK or in relation to qualifying investments traded on a prescribed market

See Section 2.4 of your Study Text

53. B   The FSA has power to prosecute for insider dealing under FSMA 2000

See Section 1.6 of your Study Text

54. A   The Joint Money Laundering Steering Group (JMLSG) Guidance Notes set out best business guidelines to comply with the Money Laundering Regulations and POCA 2002

See Section 3.8 of your Study Text

55. C   POCA 2002 is widely drafted and so covers any benefit (money or other) that has arisen from criminal conduct

See Section 3.1 of your Study Text

56. D   3% is the threshold at and above which holdings must be disclosed, when a percentage point is crossed

See Section 5.3 of your Study Text

57. C   Misleading Statements and Practices (s397) amount to a criminal offence. It is the insider dealing offence that concerns the use of unpublished information and applies only to individuals

See Section 2.13 of your Study Text

58. D   The exact term in s397 is 'relevant investments'

See Section 2.13 of your Study Text

59. A   Directors will be committing insider dealing if using confidential information obtained due to the nature of their position. The Model Code provides a set of recommendations designed to avoid suspicions of insider dealing

See Section 5.4 of your Study Text

60. B   This is the due diligence defence. The other answers are defences under Criminal Justice Act 1993

See Section 2.11 of your Study Text

61. A   An offence of insider dealing under Criminal Justice Act will be committed if there is a connection with UK – either dealing on UK markets, through a UK intermediary or the investor is a UK resident. Further, dealing would have to occur on a regulated exchange or through an intermediary. Therefore deals between private investors are not covered by the Act. The instruments not covered by the Act are commodities, currencies and their derivatives

See Section 1 of your Study Text

62. A   Disclosure to the MLRO is a defence against a charge of assistance

See Section 3.6.1 of your Study Text

63. A   The other factors can be the same for both terrorist financing and money laundering

See Section 4.1 of your Study Text

64. B The general purpose is to make sure that price-sensitive information is available to investors. The firms will make reports to Regulatory Information Services and these companies in turn will be the source of information to quote vendors. However, the FSA recognises that certain information can be detrimental to the company and its investors if disclosed and allows for disclosure to be delayed

See Section 5 of your Study Text

65. C You will have to ensure that any country outside the EEA has an adequate level of protection in relation to processing personal data

See Section 6.2 of your Study Text

66. B In A, C, and D, the companies will be subject to regulatory requirements in France, the US and Singapore respectively

See Section 8.1.3 of your Study Text

67. C Disclosure rules will be determined by the local regulator

See Section 8.3 of your Study Text

68. B If the goal of the fund manager is to push the price of the ABC shares up to increase the value of the fund, other investors can be disadvantaged by making wrong investment decisions on the basis of the artificially inflated share price. This offence is market abuse under s118 FSMA 2000

See Section 2 of your Study Text

69. B The Code of Market Conduct identifies so-called safe harbours. The issuer following the Listing Rules when disclosing information to the market will not be found to have committed market abuse

See Section 2.8 of your Study Text

70. A Remember that passporting is covered throughout the EEA and hence is broader than just the EU. FATF stands for the Financial Actions Task Force and is not a regulator

See Section 8.1.3 of your Study Text

71. C This is the best available answer. B and D describe the Markets in Financial Instruments Directive (MiFID) and A describes the Prospectus Directive

See Section 8.2 of your Study Text

72. D All of these are covered

See Section 8.2 of your Study Text

73. C The other options are core investment services but advising on mergers and acquisitions is an ancillary service

See Section 8.1.2 of your Study Text

74. B Insurance companies and credit card companies are not covered by Basel II. The CAD preceded Basel II and not the reverse. The reference to Switzerland is a pure distractor

See Section 7.2 of your Study Text

75. C The MiFID definition of financial instrument is quite wide and will include for example transferable securities, money market instruments, units in a CIS and most type of derivatives. However, currencies and direct investment in commodities are not covered by MiFID

See Section 8.1.2 of your Study Text

76. D The MiFID investment services and activities are: receiving and transmitting orders, execution of client orders, dealing on own account, managing portfolios, investment advice, underwriting and placing and operating an MTF

See Section 8.1.2 of your Study Text

77. D A broker dealer will be an investment firm. All of the others are exempt from MiFID

See Section 8.1.1 of your Study Text

78. D This is the best available description of the purpose of MiFID

See Section 8.1.1 of your Study Text

79. B UCITS III allows investment into transferable securities, money market instruments, forward contracts and financial derivatives, deposits and units in other collective investment schemes. Direct investment in gold is not permitted

See Section 8.2 of your Study Text

80. D Insurance companies, collective investment schemes and credit institutions are not engaged in MiFID business when they are not providing MiFID services

See Section 8.1.2 of your Study Text

81. D Since this is cross border business, there is no requirement for the French firm to be authorised in the UK

See Section 8.1.3 of your Study Text

4. FSA Conduct of Business and Client Assets Sourcebooks

Questions

1.   **All of the following are normally covered by the FPO exemptions, except**

   A   Investment professionals

   B   General insurance

   C   Deposits

   D   Internet sales

2.   **The FSA Financial Promotions rules cover**

   I   A financial promotion within the UK

   II   An unwritten cold call from the UK aimed at non-UK investors

   III   Issuance and approval of financial promotions within the UK

   IV   An incoming promotion from an EEA firm in respect of MiFID business

   A   I, II, III and IV

   B   II, III and IV

   C   I and III

   D   I, II and III

3.   **For a transaction that is undertaken for a retail client on 3 April**

   A   It must be confirmed by telephone by the end of the business day

   B   A confirmation must be sent by 4 April

   C   A confirmation must be sent when the customer requests it

   D   The compliance officer will retain all confirmation notes

4.   **To be classified as a High Net Worth Individual under the Financial Promotions Order requires a net income of**

   A   £100,000

   B   £250,000

   C   £48,000

   D   £120,000

5.   **The client money rules are intended to protect**

   A   Other investment firms should the firm become insolvent

   B   Shareholders should the firm become insolvent

   C   Bondholders should the firm become insolvent

   D   Clients should the firm become insolvent

6. What is the definition of client money?

A Money which the firm looks after, but which is not its own

B Money from the proceeds of a trade

C Money which the client deposits with the firm for payment of its fees

D Interest payable to all customers

7. An effective conflicts of interest policy is least likely to involve

A Policy of independence

B 'Chinese walls'

C A policy of free exchange of information between employees

D Segregation of duties

8. The COBS requirement for information to be clear, fair and not misleading applies to

A The firm communicating regulatory information to their employees

B The firm putting together a client agreement for a retail client

C The firm putting together a marketing brochure for distribution to eligible counterparties only

D The firm writing a report to the FSA

9. For a new retail client in respect of designated investment business, when must a firm provide a retail client with the terms of the agreement they are obliged to provide?

A Within five business days of starting business

B Normally before the client is bound by any agreement

C It is not necessary to provide the terms of agreement

D Immediately after the client is bound by the agreement, no matter how the agreement was concluded

10. Which pair of words best describe a 'financial promotion'?

A Advertisement/encouragement

B Incentive/publicity

C Invitation/inducement

D Prospectus/upgrade

11. Which type of information is not necessary when assessing the suitability of a client?

A Knowledge and experience

B Financial situation

C Investment objectives

D Age and proximity to retirement

12. **Which of the following is not deemed to be a reasonable non-monetary benefit with respect to the sale of packaged products?**

A Assistance in promotion of a firm's packaged products

B Reasonable travel and accommodation expenses for immediate family members

C Training facilities

D Appropriate information about software

13. **Under MiFID, one of the conditions that a retail client needs to satisfy in order to become an elective professional client is to pass a 'quantitative' test. This test consists of satisfying two requirements out of a possible three. Which of the following tests is not one of the three options?**

A The client has traded, in significant size, on the relevant market at an average frequency of ten transactions per quarter over the previous four quarters

B The client's portfolio exceeds €500,000

C The client works/has worked in financial sector for at least one year in a professional position which requires knowledge of transactions/services

D If the client is a UK-based private person they must have passed an examination of the Chartered Institute for Securities and Investment

14. **If a retail client has not requested otherwise, how often must firms send periodic statements?**

A Every month

B Quarterly

C Semi-annually

D Annually

15. **What is true about the rules on churning and switching?**

A The rules apply to all clients

B The rules permit these practices if the client agrees

C The rules apply when providing a discretionary service to a retail client

D Churning involves overtrading of packaged products

16. **An employee of an authorised firm wants to trade for themselves. Which of these statements is true?**

A The employee must trade through an account with his/her firm

B The employee must notify the MLRO of all trades that they do

C The employee does not have to use an account at his/her firm but there must be a system to enable trades to be reported to his/her firm

D The employee must hold all investments for a minimum of six weeks and is not allowed to trade shares in his/her own company

17. **Which of the following is not true in relation to the use of dealing commission?**

A   Allowable goods/services do not now include dedicated telephone lines, seminar fees and services relating to the valuation or performance measurement of portfolios

B   The rules apply where an investment manager executes customer orders through a broker and passes on the broker's charges to its customers and in return receives goods or services in addition to the execution of its customer orders

C   Allowable goods/services do not now include research

D   The rules expand on the FSA Principles of Integrity, Customers' Interests and Conflicts of Interest

18. **An independent financial adviser (IFA) sells a product on behalf of an investment firm. Which of the following is correct?**

A   It is the responsibility of the IFA to check that the information period is accurate

B   It is the responsibility of the investment firm to check that the information is accurate

C   It is the responsibility of the IFA to check that the product is suitable and of the investment firm to check that the information provided is accurate

D   The investment firm must ensure that the advice provided was suitable

19. **Suppose that a firm has received investment instructions from another firm who is acting as agent of the investor. Which of the following is or are correct?**

   I   A written agreement may treat the investor as the firm's client

   II   For designated investment business, the firm may treat the agent as client if the agent is another authorised firm

   III   For designated investment business, the firm may treat the agent as client if the agent is an overseas financial services institution

A   I only

B   I and II

C   II and III

D   I, II and III

20. **The 'website conditions' are best described as a set of**

A   Requirements governing financial promotions posted on web pages

B   Website development specifications designed to prevent 'phishing' attacks

C   Specifications to be satisfied by firms using a website to convey certain communications using electronic media

D   Security measures to prevent internet 'denial of service' attacks on financial institutions

21. **The Conduct of Business Sourcebook applies to a**

A   French company providing an insurance policy to UK based firm

B   UK re-insurance company providing services to UK firms

C   An American investment bank advising a FTSE 100 company

D   UK fund manager managing an occupational pension scheme for a Paris-based company

22. **Which one of the following can be classified as a per se professional client of a MiFID firm?**

A   A company with net assets of €1.5m and turnover of €3m

B   A company with €10m assets and €20m turnover

C   A manager of a regulated collective investment scheme

D   A large business with €20m funds to invest

---

23. **A firm is executing a client's order along with an order for its own account. Which one of the following is correct?**

A   The firm does not have to advise the client that the aggregation with an own account order is taking place

B   The aggregation is permitted provided the client has been advised that such aggregation may lead to a disadvantage

C   Aggregation is permitted if the firm is saving money on an aggregated transaction

D   Mixing client orders with orders from the firm is never permitted

---

24. **Which one of the following is correct in connection with the COBS rules on appropriateness?**

A   When the client provides a firm with a specific request not to carry out the appropriateness assessment, appropriateness obligations can be waived

B   The firm does not need to carry out appropriateness assessment for a client based overseas

C   Appropriateness assessment will need to be undertaken by a discretionary investment manager

D   Appropriateness will have to be established when executing an order relating to a direct offer financial promotion

---

25. **Appropriateness will need to be established**

A   Before every transaction

B   For every class of investments and services at the outset of the business relationship

C   For certain transactions carrying higher level of risk

D   At the start of every business relationship

---

26. **Which one of the following is correct in connection with churning and switching?**

A   Churning and switching is permitted as long as investment manager finds that strategy suitable

B   The rules apply to discretionary portfolio management

C   If separate transactions are suitable for the client, a series of those transactions are also suitable

D   The rules apply to non-advised sales of units in a regulated collective investment schemes

---

27. The personal account dealing policy will aim to prevent employees from engaging in

A Dealing in equity issued by their firm after the Board of Directors made an announcement about the profits

B Dealing on the basis of information contained in draft research reports

C Dealing in securities held on the own account of the firm

D Dealing on exchanges that are not given the status of a recognised investment exchange

28. The conflict of interest policy is least likely to prevent

A A conflict between the authorised firm and their client

B A conflict between the firm and their competitor

C A dispute between different divisions within an authorised firm

D A dispute between the clients of the firm

29. Which one of the following will be considered as client money?

A Client's cash used for settlement of a transaction following a purchase of units in a Unit Trust

B A remittance, part of which is fees due to the firm

C Money held in a deposit account with a bank

D Gold coins held for the value of the metal

30. Client money rules require the firm to

A Separate money belonging to the client from those of the firm

B Separate client money from those of other clients'

C Refer the client to the Financial Ombudsman Service when there is a discrepancy identified during reconciliation

D Report client money breaches to the FSA as soon as reasonably practicable

31. The rule on inducements

A Prevents authorised firms from making and receiving payments which can lead to avoidance of their duty to the client

B Prohibits the firm to receive any payments from third party providers

C Requires detailed disclosure of all inducements received

D Protects the interests of retail clients only

32. A direct offer financial promotion might be best described as an offer to

A Enter into an agreement with a high net worth individual without receiving further information

B Discuss an agreement with a new potential customer without receiving further information

C Investors to purchase investments directly 'off-the-page' without receiving further information

D Extend an agreement with an existing customer without receiving further information

33. **How long does a customer have to cancel units in a regulated collective investment scheme without an ISA wrapper?**

A   5 days

B   7 days

C   14 days

D   30 days

34. **Regarding information about costs and charges, which of the following would most likely not be required to be provided?**

A   Total price to be paid

B   Notice that other costs could arise

C   Warning about changing interest rates

D   Payment arrangements

35. **Which of the following is not true of unwritten financial promotions outside of the firm's premises?**

A   They may be conducted at any time of day

B   The person communicating it must identify himself and his firm

C   The person communicating it must clarify if the client wants to continue or terminate the communication

D   If an appointment is made then a contact point must be given to the client

36. **All of the following are requirements for a Key Features Document, except**

A   The keyfacts logo

B   It must contain a statement regarding the Financial Services Authority

C   It must display the firm's brand as prominently as any other

D   Provision of a list of senior management of the firm

37. **Which of the following is not considered to be an 'excluded communication' for the purposes of the Financial Promotions Order rules?**

A   Those subject to the Takeover Code

B   A personal quotation or illustration

C   A one-off promotion

D   A promotion aimed at selling a share dealing service

38. Which of the following statements about rules governing investment research activities is false?

A Financial analysts can take positions in securities contrary to their current recommendations only in exceptional circumstances and with senior permission

B Analysts must refrain from dealing on the information contained in research until the clients have been provided with time to consider it

C Research analysts must not promise issuers favourable research coverage

D The issuer should be permitted to review unpublished research on their company at any time

---

39. When a firm provides performance information in relation to MiFID business, to what period must it relate?

A The five preceding years

B If the product has been established for less than five years, then only three years data need be used

C At least the five proceeding years or the whole period of the life of the product if this is less than five years

D A twelve month period only

---

40. What is the purpose of the rules on personal account dealing?

A To prevent dealing when in the knowledge that the firm's research department are about to release a positive report on a security

B To prevent dealing in shares owned by the investment company

C To prevent dealing in shares when the company's directors have just announced the results

D To prevent the firm taking a principle position in securities where there is a conflict of interest

Answers

1. **D** Internet sales are very clearly covered by the Financial Promotions rules

   See Sections 3.9 and 3.10 of your Study Text

2. **D** Unwritten cold calls made to persons outside of the UK still require the firm to follow FSA rules

   See Sections 3.9 of your Study Text

3. **B** Confirmation notes, unless declined, must be sent no later than the first business day following receipt of confirmation (no later than **T + 1**)

   See Section 6.1 of your Study Text

4. **A** A high net worth individual is exempt from S21 of FSMA and the financial promotion rules of the Conduct of Business Sourcebook

   See Section 3.10 of your Study Text

5. **D** If client money were not protected, non-segregated funds would be seized by the liquidator and treated as the property of the firm

   See Section 7.1 of your Study Text

6. **A** This is the best definition of client money

   See Section 7.1 of your Study Text

7. **C** The procedures to protect against conflicts of interest should prevent and control exchange of information between persons involved, as and where necessary.

   See Section 5.2.3 of your Study Text

8. **B** The fair, clear and not misleading rule does not apply to eligible counterparties (although Principle 7 applies to them). The rule covers communication with customers (retail and professional) of the firm rather than internal communications and communication with other organisations

   See Section 1.2 and 3.9.4 of your Study Text

9. **B** Within five business days of starting a business (A) and no requirement to provide terms of agreement (C) are incorrect distractors. Informing the client immediately no matter when the agreement was concluded (D) is valid but only if the agreement was concluded using a means of distance communication

   See Section 2.5 of your Study Text

10. **C** The words 'invitation' and 'inducement' are those used in the FSA description

    See Section 3.9.1 of your Study Text

11. **D** It is possible that age and proximity to retirement may arise during the assessment but they are not deemed to be necessary information

    See Section 4.1 of your Study Text

12.   **B**   Although seasonal travel and accommodation expenses are acceptable for those directly involved in the transaction, no mention is made of immediate family members

See Section 5.4 of your Study Text

13.   **D**   The quantitative test does not include a requirement for clients to pass CISI exams!

See Section 2.2.3 of your Study Text

14.   **C**   Periodic statements must normally be sent to retail client six-monthly

See Section 6.2 of your Study Text

15.   **C**   Churning relates to the overtrading of investments generally whereas switching relates to the overtrading of packaged products. These rules do not protect eligible counterparties. The rule on churning would apply, for example, when providing a discretionary service to a retail client

See Section 5.12 of your Study Text

16.   **C**   Firms must keep records of all personal transactions notified by them and of any authorisation or prohibition made in connection with them. Employees do not have to use an account at their firm but there must be a system to enable trades to be reported to the employees' firm

See Section 5.11 of your Study Text

17.   **C**   Allowable goods/services still include research but do not include dedicated telephone lines, seminar fees and services relating to the valuation or performance measurement of portfolios

See Section 5.5 of your Study Text

18.   **C**   The IFA is responsible for the quality of the advice and the product provider is responsible for producing the product literature

See Section 4.1 of your Study Text

19.   **D**   These apply under the 'agent as client' rules in COBS

See Section 2.3 of your Study Text

20.   **C**   COBS requires firms delivering certain communications using electronic media to use a 'durable medium' or to use a website complying with the website conditions

See Section 1.4 of your Study Text

21.   **D**   Insurance is not a regulated activity covered by the COBS rules. It is not clear whether the American bank is based in the US or in the UK, and whether the FTSE 100 company is being advised in the UK. Pension fund management is one of the activities defined as designated investment business and the manager is based in the UK

See Section 1 of your Study Text

22.   **C**   The 20 x 40 x 2 rule for large undertakings is not satisfied in any of the examples; the fund manager is an authorised firm and therefore is by default a professional client

See Section 2.2.3 of your Study Text

23. **B** Only a general disclosure of aggregation is required, not disclosure prior to every transaction where it might happen

See Section 5.9 of your Study Text

24. **D** The firm must establish appropriateness for transactions in complex instruments regardless of where the client is based. A discretionary manager will follow the suitability rule

See Section 5.4 of your Study Text

25. **C** Appropriateness only needs to be established for transactions in complex financial instruments

See Section 4.3 of your Study Text

26. **B** B is the best answer. Dealing for some clients more frequently than for others can be considered suitable. However, if actions are classified as churning and switching, this implies that the manager is dealing more frequently than the client's investment objectives require. Non-advised sales are covered by appropriateness rules

See Section 5.12 of your Study Text

27. **B** Dealing ahead of publication of reports is prohibited as this puts the recipient of the research at a disadvantage in comparison to the employee of the firm

See Section 5.3 and 5.11 of your Study Text

28. **B** Regulatory requirements for conflicts of interest aim to protect the interests of the client

See Section 5.2 of your Study Text

29. **B** Only money held in connection with designated investment business will be considered client money, and not the contents of deposit accounts. The others are the items specifically identified by the FSA as not being client money.

See Section 7 of your Study Text

30. **A** In the event of a discrepancy, the firm is under an obligation to investigate it and to correct or make good the shortfall. If unable to correct or top up the client's account, the firm should notify the FSA without delay

See Section 7 of your Study Text

31. **A** The rule on inducements protects the interests of all clients. Only summary disclosure of fees/commissions/non-monetary benefits from third party providers are required. Detailed disclosure must be provided on request

See Section 5.4 of your Study Text

32. **C** A direct offer financial promotion must contain appropriate disclosures and for non-MiFID business additional information so that the client is reasonably able to understand the risks and make investment decisions on an informed basis

See Section 3.14 of your Study Text

33. **C** Advised and Non-life and Pensions contracts (at a distance) have the right to cancel within 14 calendar days

See Section 4.5 of your Study Text

34.   C   No mention is made in respect of changing interest rates

See Section 3.8.1 of your Study Text

35.   A   Such communications may only be conducted at an 'appropriate' time of day

See Section 3.15 of your Study Text

36.   D   A Key Features Document has many requirements but D is not one of them

See Section 4.4 of your Study Text

37.   D   The main types of excluded communication are those which benefit from a Financial Promotions Order exemption, those subject to the Takeover Code, personal quotation/illustrations and one-off financial promotions

See Section 3.9.7 of your Study Text

38.   D   Pre-publication drafts can be previewed by the issuer only for the purpose of verifying compliance

See Section 5.3 of your Study Text

39.   C   Whilst answer A is correct, it is only correct if the information or service has been in existence for five years or more. Answers B and D are simply incorrect

See Section 3.13 of your Study Text

40.   A   This is the best available answer. This is because the personal account dealing rules apply to employee trading where a conflict of interest arises

See Section 5.11 of your Study Text

5. Complaints and Redress

Questions

1. **If a complaint investigated by a firm has not been conciliated, to which of the following can the complaint be referred?**

   A   Financial Services and Markets Tribunal

   B   Financial Ombudsman Service

   C   Complaints Commissioner

   D   Financial Services Compensation Scheme

2. **What is the maximum sum of money that the Financial Services Compensation Scheme may pay out in any one year?**

   A   £10m

   B   £50m

   C   £100m

   D   No specified limit

3. **Who funds the Financial Services Compensation Scheme?**

   A   FSA

   B   Taxpayers

   C   FSA-authorised firms

   D   Government

4. **To whom is the Financial Services Compensation Scheme (FSCS) directly accountable?**

   A   The FSA

   B   HM Treasury

   C   The Lord Chancellor

   D   The Governor of the Bank of England

5. **By whom is the Financial Ombudsman Service board appointed?**

   A   The FSA

   B   The Bank of England

   C   HM Treasury

   D   The Lord Chancellor

6. **Which one of the following statements about the Financial Ombudsman Service is false?**

    A   The maximum award by the Ombudsman is £100,000 plus costs

    B   There is a registration fee and appeals process

    C   It can hear cases regarding non-regulated activities as part of its voluntary jurisdiction

    D   It is available to all clients

7. **A professional client that is a company with 25 employees has lost £80,000 owing to the negligence of an FSA-authorised firm regarding a derivatives transaction that becomes insolvent during 2010. The client would be eligible to make a maximum claim from the Financial Services Compensation Scheme of**

    A   £80,000

    B   £50,000

    C   £48,000

    D   £nil

8. **If the outcome of the Financial Ombudsman investigation is accepted by the complainant, then it is**

    A   At the discretion of the firm to comply

    B   Implemented by HM Treasury

    C   Binding on the firm

    D   Binding on the customer

9. **If the outcome of the Financial Ombudsman investigation is declined by the complainant, then the outcome**

    A   Is determined by the HM Treasury

    B   Is determined by the courts in all cases

    C   Remains binding on the firm

    D   Is not binding on the firm

10. **If a complaint has not been resolved within eight weeks, which of the following must be given to a complainant?**

    A   Information about the Financial Ombudsman Service

    B   Information about the Financial Services Authority

    C   Information about the Financial Services Compensation Scheme

    D   Information about the Office of Fair Trading

11. **To whom should an eligible complainant take his complaint first?**

A The FSA

B Financial Ombudsman Service

C The authorised firm

D The Complaints Commissioner

12. **Which of the following is true?**

A The maximum payout from the Financial Services Compensation Scheme for protected deposits is £100,000

B The maximum payout from the Financial Services Compensation Scheme for protected investments is £100,000

C The maximum fine for market abuse is £1,000,000

D The maximum award by the Financial Ombudsman Service is £100,000 plus costs

13. **A firm is required to record complaints received and report to the FSA**

A Every month

B Every six months

C Every year

D Every two years

14. **Which of the following are not individually a sufficient reason for a complainant to refer a complaint to the Financial Ombudsman?**

I The firm has issued a final response after four weeks but the complainant considers it unsatisfactory

II The firm has not sent its final response and eight weeks has elapsed since the complaint was received by the firm

III The claimed loss exceeds £100,000

A I only

B I and II

C II and III

D III only

15. **It is November 2010, Graham Bean holds accounts with the following balances at two independent authorised banks, First Elements Bank and Ratesave Bank.**

First Elements Current Account	£19,000
First Elements Saver Account	£35,000
Ratesave Instant Access	£49,000

How much in total should Graham be entitled to recover under FSCS rules if both banks fail now?

A   £48,000

B   £50,000

C   £99,000

D   £103,000

Answers

1. **B**   The Complaints Commissioner investigates complaints against the FSA itself

    See Section 2.1 of your Study Text

2. **D**   There is no maximum payout for the scheme as a whole, although there are maximum payouts for eligible claimants in each case of failure of a firm

    See Sections 3.1 and 3.3 of your Study Text

3. **C**   Authorised firms pay levies to the scheme

    See Section 3.1 of your Study Text

4. **A**   It is directly accountable to the FSA. Given that the FSA is accountable to HMT, it is indirectly accountable to the Treasury

    See Section 3.1 of your Study Text

5. **A**   The FOS Board is appointed by the FSA. It is however independent from the FSA and authorised firms

    See Section 2.2 of your Study Text

6. **D**   The FOS is not available to all clients. It is only available to eligible complainants

    See Sections 1.2, 2.2, 2.3, 2.5 of your Study Text

7. **D**   A professional client who is a large company is not an eligible claimant

    See Section 1.2 of your Study Text

8. **C**   The firm is then bound by the Ombudsman's ruling

    See Section 2.5 of your Study Text

9. **D**   If the complaining customer refuses to accept the outcome of the FOS, then it is not binding on the firm; instead, the complainant may choose to take or not to take their case to court

    See Section 2.5 of your Study Text

10. **A**   Complainants must be given the FOS leaflet and told of their right to use the service

    See Section 1.7 of your Study Text

11. **C**   The complainant must first take his complaint to the firm. If it is not resolved to his satisfaction, he may go to the Financial Ombudsman Service

    See Section 2.1 of your Study Text

12. **D**   The maximum payout for protected investments under the Compensation Scheme is £50,000 and maximum binding remedy for firms from the Ombudsman is £100,000

    See Sections 2.5 and 3.3 of your Study Text

13. **B**   The FSA requires a firm to record complaints and report to the FSA every six months the total number received, the number completed within timescales, and the total number outstanding

See Section 1.11 of your Study Text

14. **D**   Complainants must take their complaint to the firm before the FOS. Either I or II is a sufficient reason for referral to the FOS

See Section 2.1 of your Study Text

15. **C**   The limit (£50,000 in 2010) is per person per failed institution. The limit for Graham's First Elements account balances will be £50,000, and Graham should also receive 100% of the Ratesave balance of £49,000

See Section 3.3 of your Study Text

Practice
Examinations

Contents

Practice Examination 1

50 Questions in 1 Hour

1.   Which of the following are classified as investments under the Financial Services and Markets Act 2000?

        I   Swaps

        II   Forward rate agreements

        III   Floating rate notes

        IV   Commercial paper

   A   I and II

   B   I and IV

   C   II, III and IV

   D   I, II, III and IV

2.   Which of the following is true of the Bank of England?

   A   It is the regulatory authority for banks and deposit taking institutions in the UK

   B   Its Monetary Policy Committee sets official interest rates in the UK

   C   It sets the UK's inflation target

   D   Its employees are required to be approved persons under the requirements of the Financial Services and Markets Act 2000

3.   When a firm provides performance information in relation to MiFID business, what is the period it must relate to?

   A   The five preceding years

   B   If the product has been established for less than five years, then only three years data need be used

   C   At least the five preceding years or the whole period of the life of the product if this is less than five years

   D   A 12-month period only

4.   Under MiFID, if an investment firm sets up a branch in another EEA state, whose local rules will the branch have to adhere to?

   A   Home state

   B   Host state

   C   Home and host states

   D   Home or host state (the branch can choose which rules to follow)

5.   **Which two of the following does a private person need to prove in order to sue under S150 of FSMA 2000?**

   A   Negligence by the firm and criminality by the firm

   B   Criminality by the firm and breach of a rule

   C   Breach of a rule and financial loss

   D   Financial loss and negligence by the firm

6.   **Which two of the following would be a breach of the insider dealing legislation contained within the Criminal Justice Act 1993?**

   I   Selling on non-public price-sensitive information

   II   A director dealing in the shares of his own company within two months of the announcement of results

   III   A director of a company buying shares in an associated company

   IV   Purchasing on non-public price-sensitive information

   A   I and II

   B   I and IV

   C   III and IV

   D   II and III

7.   **Which of the following terms best describes the direction which the FSA currently wishes to follow in its supervision of firms?**

   A   Self-regulatory

   B   Intrusive

   C   Rule-based

   D   Light-touch

8.   **Which of the following regulated activities is included in 'Designated Investment Business'?**

   A   Advising on investments

   B   Activities related to general insurance contracts

   C   Activities relating to Funeral plans

   D   Activities relating to Lloyd's business

9.   **Which of the following is not a client category under MiFID?**

   A   Professional clients

   B   Eligible counterparties

   C   Retail clients

   D   Intermediate clients

10. **Which two of the following tests are necessary in order to treat a client as an elective professional client?**

    I   Qualitative test

    II Mandatory test

    III Quantitative test

    IV Management test

A I and II

B II and III

C I and III

D II and IV

11. **Which two of the following must a firm provide to clients in a comprehensible form?**

    I   Details of the firm and its services

    II   Costs and associated charges

    III Specifically a set of the firm's last audited accounts

    IV Specifically a list of all current directors of the firm

A I and II

B II and IV

C III and IV

D II and III

12. **With respect to the use of dealing commission, which of the following goods and services are not acceptable to the FSA?**

    I   Seminar fees

    II Employee salaries

    III Computer hardware

    IV Subscriptions for publications

A III and IV

B I, II, III and IV

C I, II and III

D II, III and IV

13. **Which of the following is true with regard to the Money Laundering regulations?**

A Records should be kept for a three-year period

B They apply to authorised firms only

C Where the client is introduced by an authorised firm, the firm can rely on the introducer for identification

D Politically exposed persons (PEPs) require simplified due diligence (SDD)

14. **Which of the following does not fall within the definition of an action covered by the Terrorism Act 2000?**

    A   Actions aimed at advancing a religious cause

    B   Actions designed to intimidate or influence a government

    C   Actions designed to intimidate the public

    D   Actions aimed at the advancement of a social cause

15. **An employee of the firm carrying out designated investment business with a client enters into a trade with an eligible counterparty using her own money. Which one of the following she must do?**

    A   Report the trade to the Market Supervision department of the FSA

    B   Inform HM Treasury

    C   Inform HMRC

    D   Follow the firm's policy on personal account dealing

16. **Which two of the following are exempt under s19 FSMA?**

    I   The English Tourist Board

    II   Tokyo Stock Exchange

    III   A company providing general insurance

    IV   International Monetary Fund

    A   I and II

    B   I and III

    C   III and IV

    D   I and IV

17. **Which of the following is the best execution rule designed to protect?**

    A   Investors generally

    B   Retail clients generally

    C   Retail and professional clients generally

    D   Retail and professional clients, but professional clients can opt out

18. **Which of the following is not true regarding the process of obtaining authorisation from the FSA?**

    A   The FSA has the right to refuse an application, in which case the applicant has no right to appeal

    B   The information required by the FSA for determining an application must be proportionate to the nature of the applicant's business

    C   If the applicant is a UK company, it must have its head and registered offices located in the UK

    D   There are five threshold conditions in COND with which the applicant must comply

19. **When must the authorised firm assess appropriateness?**

    A When executing a warrants transaction for a retail client as a result of a direct offer financial promotion

    B For a life insurance investment when the client has declined advice

    C For an authorised collective investment scheme

    D All transactions with retail clients

20. **Which of the following rules is applicable to eligible counterparties?**

    A Client categorisation

    B Best execution

    C Appropriateness

    D Client agreements

21. **Which of the following are true of the FSA's tests with regard to fitness and propriety?**

    I In considering a firm's application, the FSA will look at the directors' ability to control and direct the business

    II The FSA will look at internal controls established by the firm

    III The FSA will consider the ability of an individual, who is seeking approval to discharge their duties and pay debts as they fall due

    IV The FSA will consider a firm's ability to comply with the financial regulations on an ongoing basis

    A I, II, III and IV

    B I and III

    C III and IV

    D I and IV

22. **In order to perform a controlled function, with which of the following Statements of Principle must an approved person conform?**

    A Skill, care and diligence in management

    B Financial prudence

    C Relations with regulators

    D Integrity

23. **Which of the following is false regarding the FSA's enforcement powers?**

    A Approved persons may receive a public statement of misconduct or a financial penalty for breaching a Statement of Principle

    B Financial penalties are normally published by the FSA

    C The FSA's powers are contained in the Consumer Redress block of the FSA Handbook

    D The FSA must normally apply to a court for a restitution order

24. **Which need not be included in a direct offer financial promotion?**

  A List of execution venues

  B Nature of services provided

  C Charges and remuneration

  D Arrangements for holding client assets

25. **With respect to 'best execution criteria', which of the following characteristics does a firm not have to take into account?**

  A The client, including categorisation as retail or professional

  B The financial instruments

  C The previous day's closing price

  D The execution venues

26. **Which of the following is the best description of behaviour covered by the market abuse offence?**

  A It occurs on a prescribed market

  B It occurs in relation to qualifying investments traded on a prescribed market

  C It occurs in relation to prescribed investments traded on a qualifying market

  D It occurs on an RIE, ROIE or DIE

27. **Which of the following is not a possible penalty for misconduct which the FSA may levy against an approved person?**

  A Private censure

  B Fine

  C Withdrawal of authorisation to conduct regulated activities

  D Withdrawal of approved person status

28. **Which one of the following is true for appropriateness obligations?**

  A The firm must collect information about client's financial situation and investment objectives

  B The firm must develop a picture of client's understanding of the nature of products and risks involved

  C Appropriateness assessment must be carried out in relation to personal recommendations provided in connection with designated investment business

  D If the client insists on the execution of a transaction which firm considered inappropriate, the firm must decline to act

29. **Which of the following does not require authorisation under the Financial Services and Markets Act 2000?**

A   Publication of a tip sheet

B   Giving of investment advice by a trustee

C   Arranging deals in investments

D   Establishing a collective investment scheme

30. **Which of the following is true with respect to membership of a Recognised Investment Exchange?**

A   The member is authorised to deal in all investments

B   The member is authorised to deal in investments relating to that exchange

C   Membership confers an exemption from authorisation

D   The member is not authorised to carry out regulated activities solely due to membership

31. **Record keeping rules require storage of information on a durable medium. Which of the following would not qualify as a durable medium?**

A   A floppy disk

B   A web page

C   Paper

D   The hard disk of a computer

32. **Which of the following is not exempt from the financial promotions rules under s21 FSMA 2000?**

A   Communications with certified high net worth individuals

B   Promotions issued by a firm's appointed representatives

C   Communications with overseas recipients

D   Generic promotions

33. **Which of the following is not a factor taken into consideration when considering whether an approved person is fit and proper?**

A   Their reputation as a person who acts with honesty and integrity

B   Their experience in dealing in the securities and derivatives markets either in the UK or overseas

C   Their financial soundness in their personal financial affairs

D   Their competence for the controlled functions they will be performing within the authorised firm

34. **Which one of the following is a regulated activity under FSMA 2000?**

A   Providing advice for unregulated mortgages

B   Arranging deals in commercial property

C   Advising on investments in a newspaper article

D   Sending dematerialised instructions

35. **The FSA Code of Market Conduct contains which two of the following?**

    I   Legislation on market abuse

    II   Examples of conduct which does amount to market abuse

    III Safe harbours

    IV Definition of qualifying investments

A I and IV

B II and III

C III and IV

D II and IV

36. **Which of the following statements is true in relation to the right to sue for a breach under S150 of FSMA?**

A It gives only to retail customers the right to sue for a breach of rules

B The firm must have been negligent for the action to succeed

C There must have been a financial loss suffered

D Fraud must have been committed

37. **What is the main benefit to customers of the client money rules?**

A They require a firm to perform frequent reconciliations of client money

B They allow one client's overdraft to be netted off against the credit balance of another

C They keep customers' money segregated from the firm in the case of collapse of a bank

D They allow interest to be earned by all customers on their client money accounts

38. **Which of the following is not a statutory exception (safe harbour) to market abuse?**

A Compliance with buy-back and stabilisation regulation

B Compliance with the takeover code

C Compliance with principles

D Compliance with listing rules

39. **Which two of the following are true in relation to money laundering?**

    I   The Proceeds of Crime Act 2002 contains legislation relating to individual offences

    II   The money laundering offences cover proceeds of serious criminal conduct only

    III The offence of tipping off in the Proceeds of Crime Act 2002 is not limited to those in the regulated sector

    IV The FSA expects a firm's MLRO to be based in the UK

A I and III

B II and IV

C I and IV

D III and IV

40. **Which of the following is false regarding data protection?**

    A   Data protection legislation is set out in the Data Protection Act 1998

    B   There are eight data protection principles

    C   Breaches of the data protection legislation are punishable by two years' imprisonment and unlimited fines

    D   The data protection legislation covers electronic or manually stored data

41. **Which of the following is not part of the FSA's risk-based categorisation procedure?**

    A   Assessment of firm's impact on regulatory objectives

    B   Probability assessment of breach of regulations

    C   FSA ongoing risk assessment review

    D   Opting up to expert status

42. **Which of the following is not defined as market abuse?**

    A   Improper disclosure

    B   Discrimination

    C   Manipulating transactions

    D   Dissemination

43. **Which of the following does not fit the definition of a packaged product?**

    A   A general insurance policy

    B   A life policy

    C   A stakeholder pension scheme

    D   A unit in a collective investment scheme

44. **What is the purpose of the rules on personal account dealing?**

    A   To prevent dealing when in the knowledge that the firm's research department are about to release a positive report on a security

    B   To prevent dealing in shares owned by the investment company

    C   To prevent dealing in shares when the company's directors have just announced the results

    D   To prevent the firm taking a principle position in securities where there is a conflict of interest

45. **Under Section 21 of FSMA 2000 certain exemptions for rules on financial promotions are specified for High Net Worth investors. A High Net Worth investor is defined as an individual who has net income or assets (excluding primary residence) respectively of**

    A   £100,000 and £250,000

    B   £100,000 and £500,000

    C   £250,000 and £100,000

    D   £250,000 and £700,000

46. **Which of the following is a regulated activity?**

    A Dealing as principal on a personal account

    B Establishing a stakeholder pension scheme

    C Acting as a trustee

    D Operating an employee share scheme

47. **Which two of the following are true regarding Designated Investment Exchanges?**

    I   They are usually based overseas or international bodies

    II   The FSA ensures that their market prices are fair

    III The FSA has no authority over them

    IV   They are exempt from authorisation

    A II and III

    B I and III

    C I and IV

    D II and IV

48. **For packaged products business, the SCDD is the**

    A Service Clause and Disclosure Declaration

    B Statement of Commissions and Direct Dealing

    C Services and Costs Disclosure Document

    D Statement of Costs and Declaratory Data

49. **When is a Regulatory Decisions Committee likely to send a notice to a firm?**

    A When there has been a complaint from a customer

    B During the approval process for an employee

    C When an approved employee has breached the statements of principle for approved persons

    D When a complainant is not satisfied with the firm's resolution of a complaint

50. **What is the cancellation period in respect of life and policies?**

    A 7 calendar days

    B 14 calendar days

    C 30 business days

    D 30 calendar days

Answers

1. **D** A swap and an FRA (Forward Rate Agreement) are cash-settled contracts for difference (CFD) and therefore are regarded as investments. FRNs (Floating Rate Notes – a bond that pays a variable coupon) and Commercial Paper are both examples of tradable debt, which means they are defined as investments. You should remember that Premium Bonds and other similar NS&I products are not tradable and hence are not investments

   See Chapter 2 Section 4.4 of your Study Text

2. **B** The FSA is responsible for regulating banks and deposit institutions in the UK. The Monetary Policy Committee sets the UK official interest rate, but the Chancellor of the Exchequer/HM Treasury sets the inflation target. The Bank of England is an 'exempt person' under the terms of the Regulated Activities Order, as a central bank. Since it is exempt, its employees need not be approved persons

   See Chapter 1 Section 1.1 of your Study Text

3. **C** The other options are distractors from the true answer

   See Chapter 4 Section 3.13 of your Study Text

4. **C** If a firm has a physical presence in another EEA country, it must adhere to the local rules of that country for most of the Conduct of Business rules. However, there are a few minor exceptions, such as personal account dealing rules, that follow the home state rules

   See Chapter 3 Section 8.1.3 of your Study Text

5. **C** To sue, a rule must have been broken (not a principle or guidance note) and financial loss incurred. Section 150 covers private persons, although the examiner may instead refer to private customers

   See Chapter 1 Section 2.5 of your Study Text

6. **B** A director dealing in shares of his own company would only be a breach of the UKLA's Model Code on Director's Share Dealings. A director buying shares in an associated company would only be an offence if they were acting on inside information

   See Chapter 3 Sections 1.3 and 5.4 of your Study Text

7. **B** Since the financial turmoil of 2007-09, the regulator has chosen to take a more 'intrusive' approach to supervision

   See Chapter 1 Section 6.3 of your Study Text

8. **A** The other options are all excluded from the narrow definition of 'Designated Investment Business'

   See Chapter 4 Section 1.2 of your Study Text

9. **D** Intermediate clients is not a classification category used in COBS

   See Chapter 4 Section 2.2 of your Study Text

10. C   'Mandatory test' and 'management test' are invented terms. The qualitative test requires experience, expertise and knowledge. The quantitative test requires a certain frequency of transactions, minimum portfolio value or knowledge of transactions from professional work in the financial sector

See Chapter 4 Section 2.2.3 of your Study Text

11. A   Whilst it is possible that information on accounts and directors may be provided as part of the details of the firm, they are not specifically required

See Chapter 4 Section 3.2 of your Study Text

12. B   The list is very long and contains many items. All four of these items are unacceptable. The only acceptable use of dealing commission beyond execution services is the provision of research

See Chapter 4 Section 5.5 of your Study Text

13. C   They apply to all financial institutions and credit institutions, not just to authorised firms. Records must be kept for five years under the Money Laundering Regulations. Enhanced due diligence is generally appropriate for PEPs

See Chapter 3 Section 3.5 of your Study Text

14. D   These are all specifically referred to under the Terrorism Act 2000, apart from advancing a social cause, which is the most legitimate sounding of the options. To be an offence under the Act, these actions must also involve violence, damage, endangerment, risk to the public and/or disruption of systems

See Chapter 3 Section 4.1 of your Study Text

15. D   FSA requires authorised firms to develop a Personal Account Dealing policy and make employees aware of it. The specific actions of the employee will be detailed in that policy

See Chapter 4 Section 5.11 of your Study Text

16. D   Both the English Tourist Board and the International Monetary Fund are listed in the Financial Services and Markets Act (Exemption) Order as being exempt. The Tokyo Stock Exchange is an example of a Designated Investment Exchange (DIE), which is not exempt from the requirement to seek authorisation. A company providing general insurance would need to be authorised

See Chapter 2 Section 1.7 of your Study Text

17. C   The best execution rule is aimed at protecting both retail and professional clients. Professional clients cannot opt out of best execution. The term 'investors generally' would include eligible counterparties

See Chapter 4 Section 5.6 of your Study Text

18. A   If the FSA decides to refuse an application, the applicant may ultimately refer the matter to the Upper Tribunal (Tax and Chancery Chamber), formerly the Financial Services and Markets Tribunal. COND is the abbreviation for the part of the FSA Handbook on Threshold Conditions

See Chapter 1 Section 7.10 and Chapter 2 Sections 2.1 and 4.7 of your Study Text

19. **A**   An appropriateness check is required where firms provide MiFID investment services other than the provision of personal recommendations or managing investments and where firms arrange deals or deal in warrants or derivatives for retail clients in response to a direct offer financial promotion

See Chapter 4 Section 4.3 of your Study Text

20. **A**   Firms are required to categorise all clients as eligible counterparties, professional clients or retail clients

See Chapter 4 Section 2.2 of your Study Text

21. **A**   The FSA may consider a wide range of criteria to assess the fitness and propriety of a firm **or** individual

See Chapter 2 Sections 4.7 and 4.8 of your Study Text

22. **D**   Skill, Care and Diligence (Statement of Principle 6) applies to significant influence functions only and Financial Prudence and Relations with Regulators are Principles for Businesses, not Statements of Principles

See Chapter 1 Sections 2.3 and 3.2 of your Study Text

23. **C**   Financial penalties are normally published by the FSA via a press release, unless it would be unfair on the person receiving the penalty, or be prejudicial to the interests of consumers. The FSA's enforcement powers are contained in the Regulatory Processes block of the FSA Handbook

See Chapter 1 Section 1.4 and Chapter 2 Section 2.7 of your Study Text

24. **A**   A direct offer financial promotion must contain any necessary disclosures relevant to that offer or invitation, e.g. information about the firm and its services, information about costs and associated charges, a description of the nature and risks of the designated investment and information regarding safeguarding assets and client money

See Chapter 4 Section 3.14 of your Study Text

25. **C**   Prices can move dramatically from one day to another and so, when seeking 'best execution' today, yesterday's price is not relevant

See Chapter 4 Section 7.6 of your Study Text

26. **B**   Although 'prescribed market' is also correct, 'qualifying investments traded on a prescribed market' is the best available answer as it is more complete and precise. 'Prescribed investments on a qualifying market' is simply wrong! Market abuse covers everything traded on a prescribed market (RIE and EEA exchanges)

See Chapter 3 Section 2.4 of your Study Text

27. **C**   An approved person is an employee of an authorised firm and therefore it is the firm which would lose its authorisation, not the approved person

See Chapter 2 Sections 4.6 and 4.11 of your Study Text

28. **B**   To determine appropriateness of a transaction, the firm must establish knowledge and experience of a client. Knowledge of the financial situation and investment objectives will be relevant in an advisory/discretionary management context rather than for an execution only relationship. For personal recommendations advisors need to follow the suitability rule. If a

client insists on an inappropriate transaction the FSA rules require the firm to use its discretion 'with regard to the circumstances'

See Chapter 4 Section 4.3.1 of your Study Text

29. **B**   This is the best answer. Arranging deals in investments and establishing a collective investment scheme are defined as regulated activities. Tip sheets need to be authorised unless they are specifically within a media publication. You are not told whether the trustee is remunerated but, as it is the only plausible answer, you must assume he is **not** remunerated, therefore the giving of investment advice by a trustee is an excluded activity and, as such, does not require authorisation

See Chapter 2 Sections 4.1 and 4.3 of your Study Text

30. **D**   Only the RIE itself is exempt from the need to be authorised; membership of an RIE does not confer exemption

See Chapter 1 Section 7.4 and Chapter 2 Section 1.7 of your Study Text

31. **B**   A web page does not normally provide a permanent record

See Chapter 4 Section 1.4 of your Study Text

32. **B**   A firm is required to apply the financial promotions rules to its appointed representatives

See Chapter 4 Section 3.9.2 of your Study Text

33. **B**   Experience is **not** a requirement to show that someone is fit and proper

See Chapter 2 Section 4.10 of your Study Text

34. **D**   Unregulated mortgages and commercial property are not specified investments, activities related to them therefore will not be regulated by the FSA. Advice in a newspaper is one of the excluded activities

See Chapter 2 Sections 4.1 and 4.3 of your Study Text

35. **B**   The Code of Conduct is part of the FSA Handbook and does not contain legislation on market abuse. The legislation is contained in S118 of FSMA, which also defines the qualifying investments

See Chapter 3 Section 2.8 of your Study Text

36. **C**   The right to sue under S150 is for 'private **persons**' (rather than a retail client). There is no need to prove negligence or fraud, just a breach of the FSA rules, but financial loss must have occurred

See Chapter 1 Section 2.5 of your Study Text

37. **C**   The main purpose of the client money rules is to segregate the firm's money from client money to prevent and protect in the case of the firm's insolvency

See Chapter 4 Sections 7.1 to 7.3 of your Study Text

38. **C**   Safe harbours define conduct that does not constitute market abuse. Complying with a safe harbour is evidence of not abusing a market. However, principles are **not** sufficient

See Chapter 3 Section 2.10 of your Study Text

39.   **C**   The Proceeds of Crime Act updates and consolidates certain earlier legislation. Money laundering covers the proceeds of all crimes. The tipping off offence (S333A) applies to those in the regulated sector

See Chapter 3 Sections 3.1 to 3.7 of your Study Text

40.   **C**   Breaches of the Data Protection Act 1998 do not result in imprisonment, only fines

See Chapter 3 Sections 6.1 to 6.3 of your Study Text

41.   **D**   Opting up is part of the classification procedures, not categorisations for risk-based purposes

See Chapter 1 Section 6.1 and Chapter 2 Section 4.9 of your Study Text

42.   **B**   Discrimination is not covered by the market abuse regime

See Chapter 3 Section 2.1 of your Study Text

43.   **A**   General insurance policies are not considered to be packaged products whereas all the others are

See Chapter 4 Section 3.8.1 of your Study Text

44.   **A**   This is the best available answer. This is because the personal account dealing rules apply to employee trading where a conflict of interest arises

See Chapter 4 Section 5.11 of your Study Text

45.   **A**   The definitions are £100,000 in net income or £250,000 in net assets

See Chapter 4 Section 3.10 of your Study Text

46.   **B**   A personal account trade by an FSA firm employee will not be holding themselves out to the market. We are not told that the trustee is unremunerated. Employee share schemes are excluded

See Chapter 2 Section 4.1 and 4.3 of your Study Text

47.   **B**   The FSA has no legal power to control DIEs, to ensure they give fair prices or any other protections

See Chapter 1 Section 7.7 of your Study Text

48.   **C**   The Services and Costs Disclosure Document has the status of guidance only

See Chapter 5 Section 3.9.3 of your Study Text

49.   **C**   The RDC does not get involved with customer complaints and would only get involved with approval of employees when someone appeals against a refusal of approval

See Chapter 2 Section 2.1 of your Study Text

50.   **D**   The answer is 30 calendar days although for other products, such as cash deposit ISAs and non-life and pension contracts (sold at a distance) the period is 14 calendar days

See Chapter 4 Section 4.5 of your Study Text

Practice Examination 2

50 Questions in 1 Hour

1. **Under s71 of FSMA, what is the category of persons that can sue for damages?**

   A Clients suffering financial loss

   B Retail clients

   C Private persons

   D Experts

2. **Which of the following is true of a Multilateral Trading Facility (MTF)?**

   A It is a facility where a firm engages in multiple core investment services

   B It is a system where a firm provides services similar to those of exchanges by matching client orders

   C It is a system where a firm takes proprietary positions in a client company

   D It is a facility where a firm operates in more than one location

3. **Which of the following would be classified as regulated activities under the Financial Services and Markets Act 2000?**

       I   A company dealing as principal

       II   A daily newspaper giving investment advice

       III   A unit trust only investing in property

       IV   A trustee giving investment advice

   A I, II, III and IV

   B I, II and III

   C I, II and IV

   D III and IV

4. **In respect of a retail client, when is a suitability report required?**

   A If the firm makes a personal recommendation and the client buys or sells

   B For small life policies (less than £50 p.a.) recommended by Friendly Societies

   C For recommendations to increase regular premiums on an existing contract

   D If the firm acts as investment manager and recommends a regulated collective investment scheme

5. **An adviser has arranged an appointment with a client. What must be provided before the meeting?**

    A   A contact point

    B   A Key Features Document

    C   A fact find

    D   Terms of business

6. **Which of the following is actionable under s150 FSMA 2000?**

    A   Breach of an evidential provision

    B   Breach of guidance giving rise to a financial loss

    C   Breach of a rule with regard to a private person

    D   Breach of a principle (only) with regard to a private person

7. **Who is covered by the market abuse offence?**

    I   Lawyers

    II   Authorised firms

    III   Approved persons

    IV   Employees within an authorised firm

    A   I and II

    B   II and III

    C   III and IV

    D   I, II, III and IV

8. **Which two of the following Statements of Principle apply to all approved persons?**

    I   Deal with the regulator in an open way

    II   Skill, care and diligence in management

    III   Comply with regulatory requirements

    IV   Integrity

    A   I and II

    B   I and IV

    C   II and IV

    D   I and III

9. **The following are all exempt from obtaining authorisation to carry on regulated activities, except**

    A   Members of Lloyd's

    B   Bank of England

    C   Trustees

    D   Appointed representatives who are representatives of an authorised firm

10. **In the context of communications by electronic media, which of the following is not normally a 'durable medium'?**

    A Computer hard drive

    B Paper

    C Internet web site

    D Compact disc

11. **Which of the following is false regarding the procedure for obtaining and maintaining approval from the FSA?**

    A The criteria the FSA refer to are contained in the Threshold Conditions Sourcebook of the FSA Handbook

    B The FSA consider whether the person's reputation might have an adverse impact on the firm he/she is employed by

    C The FSA can consider any history of drug or alcohol abuse regarding their continuing ability to perform that function

    D It is the responsibility of the firm to apply for approval, not the individual candidate seeking approval

12. **When providing information about designated investments which one of the following is not the type of information that it is necessary to provide?**

    A Risks

    B Price volatility

    C Formulae in respect of calculating risks and volatility

    D Margin requirements – where applicable

13. **Which of the following are factors influencing whether the FSA will take disciplinary action against a firm or approved person?**

    I   Whether the breach was deliberate or reckless

    II   How quickly the breach was brought to the attention of the FSA

    III The previous regulatory record of the offender

    IV   The risk of loss to market users

    A None of the above

    B II and III

    C I, II, III and IV

    D I and IV

14. **Which one of the following is not an offence under S397 of the Financial Services and Markets Act 2000?**

   A   Making a deliberately misleading statement to induce a person to enter into an investment agreement

   B   Dishonestly concealing a fact to induce a person to refrain from entering into an investment agreement

   C   Making a false promise recklessly to a person to induce someone else to enter into an investment agreement

   D   Making a false statement in good faith to induce someone to enter into an investment agreement

15. **What courses of action in the criminal courts are available to a private person who has suffered a loss as a result of insider dealing?**

   A   Damages

   B   Restitution

   C   Ability to enforce the contract

   D   None of the above

16. **All of the following would be committing an offence under the Criminal Justice Act 1993 if they purchased shares in ABC plc, except**

   A   An auditor to ABC who resigned three months ago who has confidential information on the company's results

   B   A secretary to the office services manager in ABC who has seen an advance copy of an announcement to repurchase shares

   C   A non-executive director of ABC who resigned seven months ago who expects profits to show an unexpected rise when published

   D   A friend of a director of ABC who has obtained price-sensitive information from the director

17. **Which of the following is not a *per se* eligible counterparty?**

   A   Insurance company

   B   Pension fund

   C   Central bank

   D   Treasury department of a large oil company

18. **In relation to the Model Code for Director's Dealings, which of the following is true?**

   A   Companies House imposes regulations on listed company directors in the Model Code

   B   Breach of the Model Code is a criminal offence subject to two years' imprisonment and/or an unlimited fine

   C   Directors' deals may not be made for the short term

   D   No trades should be undertaken in the three months prior to the announcement of the company's results

19. **Which of the following is not true with regard to money laundering?**

    A The source of the UK Money Laundering Regulations is the EU Directive on the prevention of the use of the financial system for the purpose of money laundering

    B The Money Laundering Regulations only apply to authorised firms

    C The FSA Senior Management Arrangements, Systems and Controls rules only apply to authorised firms

    D Under the Money Laundering Regulations firms must 'know their customers' and an example of this would be to obtain information regarding the anticipated level of business and the expected origin of funds to be used by the client

20. **Which of the following statements is true regarding the COBS financial promotion rules?**

    A They do not apply to incoming communications in relation to MiFID business of an investment firm of another EEA state that is regulated under MiFID

    B They do apply to incoming communications in relation to MiFID business of an investment firm of another EEA state that is regulated under MiFID

    C The rules only apply to 'one-off' promotions

    D The rules never apply to 'one-off' promotions

21. **Which one of the following is not a specified investment?**

    A Government debt security

    B Commercial mortgage

    C Unit in a UCITS scheme

    D Life insurance policy with an investment element

22. **Which of the following is true of a Chinese wall?**

    A It is a physical barrier between departments in a firm

    B It must be present between a Corporate Finance Department and a Dealing Department

    C Its origins date from the 1905 Boxer revolt in China

    D It is a physical or administrative barrier or other internal arrangement to contain sensitive information

23. **Who has power to issue a Prohibition Order under Section 56 of FSMA 2000?**

    A The FSA

    B The courts

    C HM Treasury

    D Private persons

24. **When implementing the 'Best execution criteria' the firm must take into account all of the following characteristics, except**

   A   The client order

   B   How long the client has been a client of the firm

   C   The execution venues

   D   The financial instruments

25. **The regulated activities of dealing and managing relate to all of the following investments, except**

   A   American Depositary Receipts

   B   Bulldog bonds

   C   Global Depositary Receipts

   D   Trade bills

26. **An FSA-authorised firm**

   A   Cannot exclude liability under FSMA 2000 or the regulatory regime

   B   Can exclude liabilities under FSMA 2000 but not under FSA Handbook

   C   Can exclude liabilities under FSA Handbook but not FSMA 2000

   D   Can exclude any liabilities if the firm believes it is reasonable to do so

27. **All of the following activities require authorisation, except**

   A   Advising on buy-to-let mortgages

   B   Managing a hedge fund

   C   Managing a bond fund

   D   Arranging deals in Yankee bonds

28. **Which of the following is true?**

   A   FSA may not prosecute for market abuse if the person believed on reasonable grounds that he was not committing market abuse

   B   FSA may not impose a financial penalty if the person believed on reasonable grounds that he was not committing market abuse

   C   FSA may only impose a financial penalty if the person believed on reasonable grounds that he was not committing market abuse

   D   FSA may only issue a private warning if the person believed on reasonable grounds that he was not committing market abuse

29. **Under the Data Protection Act 1998, personal data should be kept for**

   A   An indefinite period

   B   Six years

   C   No longer than is necessary for the purpose

   D   At least three years

30. **In which of the following circumstances is a cold (unsolicited) call allowed?**

    The call is envisaged by the recipient and

    A   A derivatives trading service is being offered

    B   A warrants fund is being sold

    C   The purpose is to discuss using derivatives to hedge an existing position with an execution-only customer

    D   The recipient already has an established client relationship

31. **When giving advice to an elective professional client the firm should, at the minimum, take account of**

    A   Investment objectives

    B   Investment objectives and financial position

    C   Investment objectives and knowledge and experience

    D   Investment objectives, financial position and knowledge and experience

32. **All of the following are powers available to the FSA if it has found that a person has engaged in market abuse, except**   *civi1 offence - No Imprisonment*

    A   The FSA may impose a maximum penalty of two years' imprisonment and an unlimited fine

    B   The FSA may make a public statement that a person has engaged in market abuse

    C   The FSA may ask the court to impose a restitution order

    D   The FSA may ask the court to impose an injunction

33. **Which of the following is not a requirement of SYSC?**

    A   Apportionment of responsibilities so that they can be monitored and controlled by directors

    B   Allocation of one or more individuals in the functions of dealing with the apportionment and overseeing the establishment of systems and controls

    C   Maintaining appropriate systems and controls

    D   The firm must always have a separate risk assessment function

34. **Which of the following would not be a disciplinary offence for an FSA approved person?**

    A   Reporting the firm to the FSA for a breach of a rule

    B   A failure to comply with a requirement of a personal account notice

    C   Provision of false information to FSA

    D   A failure to comply with the Proceeds of Crime Act 2002

35. **Which of the following activities does not require FSA authorisation?**

    A   Advising the Depository of an ICVC

    B   Advising on car loans

    C   Issuing car insurance policies

    D   Dealing in shares in a Swiss company

36. **To whom will the FSA refer a case for enforcement action?**

    A Upper Tribunal (Tax and Chancery Chamber)

    B Financial Ombudsman Service

    C FSA Enforcement Office

    D Regulatory Decisions Committee

37. **Which one of the following is a statutory objective of the FSA?**

    A To ensure the firms and individuals are registered with the FSA

    B To ensure enforcement for breaches of money laundering regulations

    C To promote public understanding of financial system

    D To enforce Criminal Justice Act 1993

38. **For MiFID business, which of the following could be classified as a professional client?**

    A A company with own funds of €2,000,000 and turnover of €15,000,000

    B A fund manager authorised by the FSA

    C A company with a balance sheet of €20,000,000 and turnover of €15,000,000

    D A company with own funds of €5,000,000 and balance sheet of €15,000,000

39. **Which of the following rules will apply to the firm's relationship with eligible counterparties?**

    A Client agreements

    B Appropriateness

    C Best execution

    D Client categorisation

40. **What is the effect of passporting?**

    A It allows member firms of the EEA who have authorisation in one country to passport their business to another EEA country, subject to the restrictions of the FSA

    B It allows member firms of the EEA who have authorisation in one country to passport their business to another EEA country, subject to the restrictions of the MiFID

    C It allows member firms of the EU who have authorisation in one country to passport their business to another EU country, subject to the restrictions of the MiFID

    D It allows member firms of the EU who have authorisation in one country to passport their business to another EU country, subject to the restrictions of the FSA

41. **If a professional client requests to opt down to be afforded greater protection in its dealings with the firm, which one of the following applies?**

    A The professional client can be treated as a retail customer without notification

    B The professional client can be categorised as a retail customer but must be notified by the firm

    C The professional client cannot opt down

    D The firm must pay attention to the experience, expertise and knowledge of the client before deciding if the client can opt down

42. **Which of the following ways of communicating with a client are not subject to the COBS rules on making recordings?**

   A   A handwritten message sent by fax

   B   An exchange of email messages

   C   An instant messaging dialogue

   D   A mobile 'phone conversation

43. **Under the rules on financial promotions, which of the following should be approved in advance?**

   A   A client meeting

   B   A billboard advert

   C   A web conference

   D   A telephone call

44. **The client assets rules (CASS) apply to**

   A   An Open Ended Investment Company (OEIC)

   B   An incoming EEA investment firm, in respect of its passported activities

   C   Non-mainstream regulated activities of an athorised professional firm

   D   Assets of eligible counterparties

45. **Which of the following is a specified investment?**

   A   Premium Bonds

   B   Trade Bills

   C   Real estate

   D   T-Bills

46. **Which of the following is true of insider dealing legislation in the Criminal Justice Act 1993?**

   A   It is not an offence for directors to undertake short-term deals in their own company's shares

   B   An insider who discloses inside information (other than in the normal course of business) is not committing an offence

   C   UK equities, gilts and related derivatives are all covered by the legislation

   D   The conduct must fall short of the standard expected by a regular user

47. **Which of the following is the maximum penalty in the Crown Court for a breach of the requirement of the Data Protection Act 1998?**

   A   Maximum fine of £5,000

   B   Unlimited fine

   C   Two years' imprisonment and an unlimited fine

   D   Six months' imprisonment and a fine of £5,000

48. **Which of the following Statements of Principle apply to all approved persons?**

   A   Compliance with regulatory requirements

   B   Skill, care and diligence in management

   C   Proper organisation of business

   D   Proper standard of market conduct

49. **What can a firm use dealing commission for?**

   A   Performance measurement analytics

   B   Seminar fees

   C   Research which provides original insight

   D   Dedicated telephone lines

50. **Under the Model Code, who are directors recommended to seek approval from before trading in the securities of their firm?**

   A   CEO

   B   Chairman

   C   Compliance Director

   D   Finance Director

Answers

1. **C** Section 71 gives a private person the right to sue a firm for damages if they suffer financial loss through an employee of an FSA firm who should have been an approved person

    See Chapter 2 Section 2.8 of your Study Text

2. **B** A multilateral trading facility provides an alternative order matching system to an exchange. The client orders match with other clients so the firm operating the system does not take proprietary positions

    See Chapter 1 Section 7.8 of your Study Text

3. **D** A company dealing as principal and a newspaper giving investment advice are **excluded activities**. Note: by 'company', this question means a non-authorised firm. Trustees are only excluded if they do not hold themselves out to the public as giving investment advice and are not separately remunerated. As a collective investment scheme, operating a unit trust is a regulated activity regardless of the underlying investment

    See Chapter 2 Sections 4.1 and 4.3 of your Study Text

4. **A** There are a number of situations when a suitability report is required – this being one of them

    See Chapter 4 Section 4.1 of your Study Text

5. **A** The financial promotions rules on unwritten promotions requires an adviser to give the client a contact point if an appointment is made

    See Chapter 4 Section 3.15 of your Study Text

6. **C** Section 150 is the right of a **private person** to sue for a breach of rules (not evidential provisions, principles or guidance notes) resulting in a financial loss

    See Chapter 2 Section 2.8 of your Study Text

7. **D** Market abuse covers just about everyone

    See Chapter 3 Section 2.1 of your Study Text

8. **B** Skill, Care and Diligence and Complying with Regulatory Requirements only apply to approved persons carrying out significant influence functions

    See Chapter 1 Section 3.2 of your Study Text

9. **C** The other options are always **exempt**. Trustees are not exempt, but rather are **excluded activities** when they are not remunerated

    See Chapter 2 Sections 1.7 and 4.3 of your Study Text

10. **C** A 'durable medium' means one that can be stored and looked at again at a later date

    See Chapter 4 Section 1.4 of your Study Text

11. **A** The criteria for an employee being approved are in the 'Fit and Proper' sourcebook of the FSA Handbook. Threshold Conditions relates to conditions the firm must establish to obtain **authorisation** from the FSA

    See Chapter 2 Sections 4.7 and 4.10 of your Study Text

12. C The other options are requirements but there is no requirement to provide formulae

See Chapter 4 Section 3.3 of your Study Text

13. C The FSA will take a wide variety of factors into account

See Chapter 2 Section 2.5 of your Study Text

14. D To breach s397 of FSMA 2000, behaviour must be **dishonest or reckless**. 'In good faith' means it was neither dishonest nor reckless, therefore **not** a breach of s397

See Chapter 2 Section 5 of your Study Text

15. D The other options are all **civil** remedies not available in criminal courts. A criminal prosecution of insider dealing, and other types of financial crime, would be undertaken by the FSA. If a private person can prove there has been a breach of an FSA rule, they could pursue the other options in the civil courts, not criminal courts

See Chapter 3 Section 1.6 of your Study Text

16. C To be an **insider**, one must have **inside information** (unpublished, price-sensitive, specific, precise information on equity, debt and related products) from an **inside source** (directly or indirectly). Once an insider, it is then an offence to deal or encourage others to deal on the basis of the information or to disclose the information unless there is a suitable defence. The auditor, the Secretary and the director's friend are clearly insiders and so, if they were to purchase shares, they would be committing an offence. A non-executive director who resigned seven months ago who expects profits to show an unexpected rise is too vague; the individual might be basing his decision on his own personal analysis rather than on inside information. As such, it is unlikely to be an offence

See Chapter 3 Sections 1.1 to 1.3 of your Study Text

17. D All the others are included in the list of *per se* eligible counterparties. A large oil company is simply a large company and is not included

See Chapter 4 Section 2.2.4 of your Study Text

18. C The Model Code is imposed by the UK Listing Authority, not Companies House. Breach is **not** a criminal offence as it is a code and not part of the general criminal law. No trades should be undertaken in the two months prior to the announcement of results

See Chapter 3 Section 5.4 of your Study Text

19. B The Money Laundering Regulations apply to a wide variety of financial institutions, not just authorised firms. An example of this is that it applies to bureaux de change who are not authorised firms. The FSA Senior Management Arrangements, Systems and Controls (SYSC) rules are contained in the FSA's Handbook and thus only apply to FSA firms

See Chapter 3 Sections 3.4, 3.5 and 3.7 of your Study Text

20. A The other options are distractors from the correct answer

See Chapter 4 Section 3 of your Study Text

21. B Commercial mortgages are not specified investments

See Chapter 2 Section 4.4 of your Study Text

22. **D** A Chinese wall is not necessarily a physical partition although it can be. It is a possible arrangement but not compulsory as the firm may have other ways of managing conflicts of interest

See Chapter 4 Section 5.2.4 of your Study Text

23. **A** The FSA has the power to issue a Prohibition Order, which prohibits an individual from being employed in the financial services industry

See Chapter 2 Section 2.7 of your Study Text

24. **B** The other options are indeed correct but the length of time a client has been a client of the firm is not relevant

See Chapter 4 Section 5.6 of your Study Text

25. **D** Trade bills are not within the definition of a specified investment. ADRs and GDRs are simply alternative ways of holding underlying securities. Bulldog bonds are listed in the UK, but issued by a non-UK company

See Chapter 2 Sections 4.1 and 4.4 of your Study Text

26. **A** Regulatory liabilities cannot be excluded

See Chapter 1 Sections 8.1 and 8.2 of your Study Text

27. **A** Advising on buy-to-let mortgages is not a regulated activity. Such mortgages are not regulated mortgage contracts and so are not specified investments

See Chapter 2 Section 4.1 of your Study Text

28. **B** This provides the best definition of what is called the due diligence defence. If a person believed on reasonable grounds that they were not committing an offence, or had taken all reasonable precautions to avoid committing an offence, the FSA may not impose a financial penalty. The FSA could still seek restitution, injunction orders and publicly censure them, but they could not fine them

See Chapter 3 Section 2.11 of your Study Text

29. **C** Principle 5 of the Data Protection Act 1998 states that personal data processed for any purpose shall not be kept for longer than is necessary for that purpose

See Chapter 3 Section 6.2 of your Study Text

30. **D** Cold/unsolicited calls are not allowed unless an existing customer envisages the call or the call relates to generally marketable packaged products or it relates to a controlled activity/service regarding readily realisable securities

See Chapter 4 Section 3.15 of your Study Text

31. **B** The suitability rules require firms to take account of the client's knowledge and experience, financial position and investment objectives. However, when advising a professional client the firm is entitled to assume that the client has the necessary experience and knowledge in that particular area. Therefore, the firm would only need to take account of the client's investment objectives and financial position

See Chapter 4 Section 4.1 of your Study Text

32. **A**   Market abuse is a civil offence and, as such, cannot result in imprisonment

See Chapter 3 Section 2.1 of your Study Text

33. **D**   **SYSC** refers to Senior Management Arrangements, Systems and Controls (in Block 1 of the Handbook). A firm must have proper apportionment records and oversight. Whilst the FSA recommends that firms might want to have a separate risk management function, it is **not mandatory**

See Chapter 1 Sections 5.1 and 5.2 of your Study Text

34. **A**   All items could lead to private censure, public censure, unlimited fines, temporary withdrawal of approval and/or permanent withdrawal of approval, except A, which is allowed under the Public Interest Disclosure Act 1998 in relation to whistleblowing. Under S56 FSMA 2000, the FSA could also prohibit any person from being employed in the financial services industry

See Chapter 2 Sections 2.7, 3 and 4.18 of your Study Text

35. **B**   Advising on car loans is not covered by the Regulated Activities Order. An ICVC is an Investment Company with Variable Capital, a form of collective investment scheme

See Chapter 2 Section 4.1 of your Study Text

36. **D**   The FSA will present the findings of their investigation to the RDC. The Tribunal is the body to which a firm or approved person may appeal about a Decision Notice from the RDC

See Chapter 2 Section 2.1 of your Study Text

37. **C**   The statutory objectives of the FSA are often examined

See Chapter 1 Section 1.3 of your Study Text

38. **B**   Authorised firms are automatically per se professional clients. For MiFID business, a company must meet any two of the following tests to be a large undertaking: €20m balance sheet, €40m turnover, €2m own funds

See Chapter 4 Section 2.2.3 of your Study Text

39. **D**   All other rules apply to retail and professional clients only

See Chapter 4 Section 2.2 of your Study Text

40. **B**   Passporting covers the **EEA** (EU plus certain other countries) and its use is defined by MiFID (Markets in Financial Instruments Directive)

See Chapter 3 Section 8.1.3 of your Study Text

41. **B**   If a professional client requests to opt down, then the firm must allow this

See Chapter 4 Section 2.3 of your Study Text

42. **D**   Mobile 'phone calls are excluded from the recording rules

See Chapter 4 Sections 1.5 of your Study Text

43. **B**   A billboard advertisement is able to be checked beforehand, so it should be approved

See Chapter 4 Section 3.17 of your Study Text

44. **D** Unlike most COBS rules, the CASS rules apply to eligible counterparties

See Chapter 4 Sections 7.1 and 7.10 of your Study Text

45. **D** Premium Bonds are National Savings & Investments products and are exempt. Trade bills, such as cheques and bills of exchange, are excluded from the definition, as is buying real estate or land

See Chapter 2 Section 4.4 of your Study Text

46. **C** Short-term deals by directors are dealt with under the UKLA – Model Code for Directors' Dealing. Conduct falling short of the standard expected by a regular market user is dealt with under FSMA s119 on market abuse

See Chapter 3 Section 1.2 of your Study Text

47. **B** A £5,000 fine is the maximum penalty in the Magistrates' Court. There is no prison sentence applicable to breaches of the DPA 1998

See Chapter 3 Section 6.3 of your Study Text

48. **D** Proper standards of market conduct apply to all approved persons. The other three only apply to significant influence functions

See Chapter 1 Section 3.2 of your Study Text

49. **C** Research is the only permitted use of dealing commission beyond execution services

See Chapter 4 Section 5.4 of your Study Text

50. **B** Directors ask the Chairman. The Chairman would ask any nominated director, usually the Chief Executive Officer

See Chapter 3 Section 5.4 of your Study Text

Practice Examination 3

50 Questions in 1 Hour

1. **Which of the following is not a specified investment under FSMA 2000?**

    A Gilt repos

    B Spot foreign exchange

    C Deposits

    D Spread betting

2. **Which of the following is not a direct power available for the FSA to use where it considers appropriate?**

    A The ability to prohibit carrying out specified functions

    B The ability to issue public censures for misconduct

    C The ability to issue a winding up order

    D The ability to seek injunctions and restitution orders

3. **Which of the following would be committing an offence under the Criminal Justice Act 1993 if they purchased shares in ABC plc?**

    A A market maker who obtained price-sensitive information in the course of his business and the information is of a kind it would be reasonable to expect him to obtain

    B A director of ABC plc with price-sensitive information who undertook the transaction intending to make a profit or to avoid a loss

    C A friend of a director of ABC plc who obtained information but was unaware that it was price-sensitive

    D An employee of ABC who has heard a rumour of an impending takeover bid

4. **Which of the following is not a power available to the FSA if it has found that a person has engaged in market abuse?**

    A The FSA may impose a maximum fine of £100,000

    B The FSA may make a public statement that a person has engaged in market abuse

    C The FSA may ask the court to impose a restitution order

    D The FSA may ask the court to impose an injunction

5. **Under the client money rules, what is the phrase used to describe a situation where a firm leaves some of its own money in a client money account?**

    A Pollution of client money account

    B Pollution of trust

    C Account in excess

    D Unreconciled account

6. **Under the EU Prospectus Directive (a) who or what is responsible for specifying the content of prospectuses and (b) who or what approves the prospectus?**

    A   (a) The company coming to market (b) The CEO of the company

    B   (a) The Prospectus Directive (b) The competent authority

    C   (a) The Prospectus Directive (b) The CEO of the company

    D   (a) The competent authority (b) The Prospectus Directive

7. **Which of the following is true of Designated Professional Bodies (DPBs)?**

    A   All UK professional bodies have DPB status

    B   Membership of a DPB gives authorisation to conduct regulated activities

    C   Exemption for members of DPBs is only allowable where the regulated activities carried out are incidental to the main business of the professional, which is not an FSMA regulated activity

    D   DPBs must follow the FSA rules

8. **Where a website is used for communication, which of the following would not be a satisfactory condition?**

    A   The provision of information to a website is appropriate to the context of the business between the firm and the client

    B   The client must specifically consent to the provision of that information in that form

    C   The website must be managed from the home state

    D   The information must be up to date

9. **In the context of appropriateness, which of the following statements is true?**

    A   The firm must assess the client's understanding of risk

    B   The rule applies when a client responds to a promotion selling non-complex instruments

    C   The firm must assess the client's financial situation and investment objectives

    D   The firm must not perform a transaction if they have not satisfied themselves that the instrument is appropriate

10. **Which of the following is correct in relation to a personal recommendation regarding a designated investment where the client has refused to provide the information necessary to assess suitability?**

    A   The investment manager may only proceed if it is for a professional client who has given express consent

    B   The investment manager should contact the FSA

    C   The investment manager may proceed if specific risk warnings are given to all clients

    D   The investment manager should decline to act

11. **What, in relation to MiFID, would be deemed to be a 'large undertaking'?**

A €20m balance sheet, €20m net turnover

B €20m balance sheet, €40m net turnover

C €20m balance sheet, €1m own funds

D €40m balance sheet, €30m net turnover

12. **Who may a firm not treat as an agent when representing his client, in respect of designated investment business?**

A Another authorised firm

B An overseas financial institution

C Another person, provided duties to the agent's client are not avoided

D Another person where the nature of the relationship between that person and his client is not clear

13. **If a firm holds designated investments or client money for a retail client – subject to MiFID custody and client money rules – it must provide all of the following information, except**

A The fact that investments or client money may be held by a third party

B The consequences for the client of the insolvency of the third party

C Client rights relating to accounts subject to jurisdiction outside of the EEA

D The rate of interest that will be paid on client money

14. **Of the following, who is not covered by the approved persons regime?**

A Systems and controls function

B Significant management function

C Customer function

D Head of a product group

15. **Which two conditions must apply when a firm has to resort to reliance on others?**

I   The third party must be an approved person

II   The third party must not be connected to the firm

III The third party must be competent

IV   The third party must reside in the UK

A I and II

B II and III

C III and IV

D I and IV

16. **You have client money held on trust with an approved bank and discover that there is excess money in this account. If the firm is declared insolvent**

   A   The client money remains safe

   B   The excess becomes due to the creditors of the bank

   C   This is a pollution of trust and the whole account becomes payable to the general creditors of the bank

   D   The firm must withdraw the excess within three business days

17. **What is the maximum penalty for a breach of Section 21 of FSMA 2000 (financial promotions)?**

   A   Six months' imprisonment and/or £5,000 fine

   B   Two years' imprisonment and an unlimited fine

   C   This is a non-imprisonable offence

   D   £5,000

18. **Which one of the following transactions do not have to be reported to the firm under personal account dealing regulatory requirements?**

   A   Purchase of shares through a broker on LSE

   B   Transactions under a discretionary management agreement

   C   Purchase of shares in a Self Invested Personal Pension

   D   Purchase of shares through a broker on NYSE

19. **Which of the following is false regarding the notices that can be issued by the FSA or the Regulatory Decisions Committee (RDC) under FSMA?**

   A   A Warning Notice sets out the case the RDC proposes to hear

   B   A Notice of Termination is issued where proceedings are no longer to be continued

   C   A Final Notice sets out action the FSA or RDC has decided to take and the date from which it takes effect

   D   The Decision Notice that the FSA or RDC can issue is a statutory notice

20. **In which of the following circumstances can a non-authorised firm communicate a financial promotion?**

   A   By having the promotion drawn up by a professional designer

   B   By discussing the promotion with an authorised firm

   C   By having an authorised firm approve the promotion

   D   No special circumstances are necessary

21. **Which of the following does not describe one of the recommendations of the Turner Review regarding the financial sector?**

     There should be:

     A   A 'lighter touch' supervisory regime

     B   Greater focus on system-wide risks

     C   Remuneration policies that discourage excessive risk-taking

     D   A new European regulatory authority

22. **Which of the following is not an exempt person under FSMA 2000?**

     A   International Monetary Fund

     B   Recognised Investment Exchange

     C   Enterprise Investment Scheme

     D   Designated Investment Exchange

23. **Which of the following statements distinguishes the concepts of 'suitability' and 'appropriateness' in respect of investment advice?**

     A   There is no difference as they are both required protections for retail clients

     B   'Suitability' involves making a personal recommendation and this is not necessarily the case with 'appropriateness'

     C   'Appropriateness' applies only to professional clients

     D   'Suitability' only applies to dealing in derivatives or warrants for a retail client

24. **Where a firm makes a research recommendation, it must make disclosures in relation to all of the following, except**

     A   All relationships and circumstances that may reasonably be expected to impair the objectivity of the recommendation

     B   Whether employees involved have remuneration tied to investment banking transactions

     C   Shareholding held by the issuer of over 3% of the share capital of the recommending firm

     D   The names of those individuals involved in preparing the research

25. **Which of the following does not describe the manner in which a firm should execute client orders?**

     A   By the end of the trading day

     B   Promptly

     C   Fairly

     D   Expeditiously

26. If a firm were to discriminate against an employee making a disclosure under the 'whistleblowing' procedures, which threshold condition may be deemed to have been breached?

A Legal status

B Suitability

C Close links

D Adequate resources

27. Where a firm is applying for authorisation from the FSA, the FSA may have regard to any person who is 'connected' to the applicant. All of the following will be deemed to be 'connected', except

A A major client of the applicant

B Any company in the same group as the applicant

C Someone who controls the applicant, i.e. owns 20% or more of the shares, or who is able to exercise a significant influence over the firm's management

D The directors and partners of the applicant

28. Under the FSA's Senior Management Arrangements, Systems and Controls rules regarding financial crime a firm should ensure the systems and controls include all of the following, except

A Appropriate measures to ensure money laundering risk is taken into account in its day to day operation

B Appropriate documentation of its risk management policies

C Appropriate provision of information to its governing body and senior management

D Appropriate measures to deny access to its services to potential customers who cannot reasonably be expected to produce detailed evidence of identity

29. When considering honesty, integrity and reputation, which is true in relation to the Rehabilitation of Offenders Act 1974?

A Only takes into account if convicted in last ten years

B Only takes into account if convicted in last five years

C Will not take into account spent convictions under any circumstances

D May take into account spent convictions if relevant

30. Firms should maintain a permanent, independent and effective compliance function.' This is

A Mandatory for common platform firms; mandatory for non-MiFID firms

B Mandatory for common platform firms; guidance for non-MiFID firms

C Guidance for common platform firms; mandatory for non-MiFID firms

D Guidance for common platform firms; guidance for non-MiFID firms

31. **Which of the following is false in relation to the anti-money laundering provisions contained within the SYSC, FSMA and the Proceeds of Crime Act?**

A   It is a requirement on firms to properly train their staff in recognising and reporting suspicions of money laundering

B   The FSA has a statutory objective to reduce the incidence of financial crime, such as money laundering

C   A firm is required to retain its records of financial transactions for anti-money laundering purposes for a period of three years ^{7}.

D   A firm does not have to verify the identity of a client in an occasional transaction unless it exceeds €15,000

32. **Which of the following is the FSA not empowered to do?**

A   Enter a firm's premises without notice

B   Interview any director, partner or employee of the firm, whether they are an approved person or not

C   Remove any documents from the firm's business premises

D   Monitor any firm on a periodic basis

33. **What is the name given to the following set of procedures?**

(1)   Identifying the customer and verifying his identity

(2)   Identifying the beneficial owner (taking measures to understand the ownership and control structure, in the case of a company or trust) and verifying his identity

(3)   Obtaining information on the purpose and intended nature of the business relationship

A   Know Your Customer

B   Customer Due Diligence

C   Enhanced Due Diligence

D   Simplified Due Diligence

34. **An investor's change in shareholding in a listed UK company must be publicised if the change in voting rights is**

A   From 0% to 1.0%

B   From 2.9% to 1.7%   *¹ ·²*

C   From 5.9% to 6.1%   *○ ²*

D   From 6.8% to 6.1%   *○ ⁾*

35. **Under the FSA rules, what is the status of an electronic communication?**

A   A firm may use electronic communications, but must follow it up with a formal paper communication

B   It is the equivalent of communicating in writing

C   It is not sufficient to only send an electronic communication

D   The firm may insist on only communicating via electronic channels

36. **Which of the following is not an investment under the Regulated Activities Order (as amended)?**

   A Ordinary shares

   B Trade bills

   C Corporate bonds

   D Treasury bills

37. **Which of the following notices allow a firm or approved person to appeal to the Upper Tribunal (Tax and Chancery Chamber)?**

   A Warning Notice only

   B Decision Notice and Supervisory Notice only

   C Decision Notice and Final Notice only

   D Decision Notice only

38. **All of the following are formal disciplinary penalties which the Regulatory Decisions Committee of the FSA may impose on an approved person, except**

   A Private warning

   B Public censure

   C Withdrawal of approval

   D Financial penalty

39. **Which one of the following statements concerning the Regulatory Decisions Committee is true?**

   A All members of the committee are FSA employees

   B It is separate from the management of the FSA

   C It is funded by the government

   D It is a statutory body

40. **All of the following are defined as regulated activities under the Financial Services and Markets Act 2000, except**

   A Dealing in investments

   B Establishing or operating a collective investment scheme

   C Managing a property portfolio

   D Advising on investments

41. **Which of the following are acts of misconduct?**

    I   Breach of FSMA 2000

    II   Failure to comply with a personal account notice

    III Provision of inaccurate information to the FSA

    IV   An act which causes another approved person to be in breach of the rules of the FSA

    A   I and IV

    B   II, III and IV

    C   I, II, III and IV

    D   I and II

42. **Which of the following is not true of a Recognised Overseas Investment Exchange?**

    A   Membership does not confer authorisation to do regulated activities

    B   Membership provides a market place in which buyers and sellers may trade

    C   They are recognised by the Treasury

    D   They regulate the conduct of participants towards each other

43. **Under s45 of FSMA, the FSA may vary a firm's Part IV permission in all of the following circumstances, except which one?**

    A   The firm is failing or is likely to fail to meet the threshold conditions for one or more of the regulated activities for which it has Part IV permission

    B   The firm's activities have come to an end and it has not applied for its permissions to be cancelled

    C   The firm has not carried out a regulated activity for which it has Part IV permission for at least 12 months

    D   It is desirable to protect customers

44. **Which one of the following is not covered by insider dealing legislation?**

    A   Debentures

    B   Foreign exchange transactions

    C   Shares

    D   Bonds

45. **With respect to the Joint Money Laundering Steering Group, which one of the following is true?**

    A   Firms must follow the guidance provided

    B   The adherence to guidance will be looked upon favourably in the event of an investigation

    C   The JMLSG has the power to impose fines

    D   JMLSG guidance only relates to individuals

46. **What is the maximum penalty for failing to report terrorism?**

    A   Two years' imprisonment and an unlimited fine

    B   Five years' imprisonment and an unlimited fine

    C   Seven years' imprisonment and an unlimited fine

    D   Fourteen years' imprisonment and an unlimited fine

47. **Under the Data Protection Act, how long must personal data records be kept for?**

    A   Three years

    B   Six years

    C   Indefinitely

    D   No longer than necessary

48. **When advising on derivative products, in what circumstances must the firm take reasonable steps to ensure the customer understands the risks?**

    A   Retail clients only

    B   Retail and professional clients

    C   When acting as investment manager

    D   When providing a personal recommendation in respect of a designated investment

49. **Which one of the following is true in connection with the FSA's Principles for Business?**

    A   Will apply to all authorised firms to the same extent

    B   Following the breach of a principle, the penalty will apply automatically

    C   Following the breach of a principle, the FSA will have to prove the firm has been at fault

    D   Customers of the firm will be able to take action against the firm following the breach of Principles

50. **Which of the following statements is true in relation to s397 FSMA?**

    A   It is a civil offence which carries a maximum penalty of an unlimited fine

    B   It only covers individuals

    C   It is an offence to mislead the market either through a statement, promise or forecast

    D   It is an offence to use unpublished price sensitive information

Answers

1. **B** Other exceptions are commodities (e.g. gold), property, National Savings & Investments products (e.g. Premium Bonds and Savings Certificates) and futures for commercial purposes

    See Chapter 2 Section 4.1 of your Study Text

2. **C** The FSA itself does not have the direct power to issue a winding up order, but must seek one from a court. Additionally, the FSA has the direct power to issue private censure, unlimited fines and withdrawal of authorisation

    See Chapter 2 Section 2.7 of your Study Text

3. **B** An insider must **knowingly** have **inside information** (i.e. specific, precise, price sensitive and not public) from a known **inside source**. Being a market maker and not intending to make a profit are acceptable defences. Other defences available are:

    ■ Believing the information was published
    ■ The investor would have dealt in the same way without the inside information
    ■ Stabilisation and market information

    See Chapter 3 Section 1.2 of your Study Text

4. **A** The FSA can ask the Court to impose an injunction, restitution or other penalty such as an **unlimited** fine. As a civil offence, however, no prison sentences can be imposed for market abuse

    See Chapter 3 Section 2.9 of your Study Text

5. **B** The other options are fictitious and the term used is 'pollution of trust'

    See Chapter 4 Section 7.3 of your Study Text

6. **B** This is a matter of getting the correct combination – and it is the Prospectus Directive and the Competent Authority

    See Chapter 3 Section 8.3 of your Study Text

7. **C** Only lawyers, accountants and actuaries are regulated by DPBs. Membership of a DPB does not give authorisation for regulated activities. These professionals will follow the rules of their relevant Designated Professional Body

    See Chapter 2 Section 1.7 of your Study Text

8. **C** There is no requirement regarding from where the web site must be managed

    See Chapter 4 Section 1.4 of your Study Text

9. **A** The aim of the appropriateness check is to determine whether the client has the experience and knowledge to be able to understand the risks involved

    See Chapter 4 Section 4.3.1 of your Study Text

10. **D** If the firm does not obtain the information it needs to be able to comply with the suitability rule, it must not make a personal recommendation to the client or take a decision to trade for them

   See Chapter 4 Section 4.1 of your Study Text

11. **B** A large undertaking meets two out of the following three:

   ■ €20m balance sheet
   ■ €40m turnover
   ■ €2m own funds

   See Chapter 4 Section 2.2.3 of your Study Text

12. **D** The other options are clearly set out in the COBS rules whereas the unclear relationship introduces some ambiguity such that the firm may not know if duties to the agent's client are being met

   See Chapter 4 Section 2.4 of your Study Text

13. **D** There is no requirement for the firm to give any information on interest that might be paid on client money

   See Chapter 4 Section 7 of your Study Text

14. **D** The Supervision Manual contains the list of controlled functions. All of the items are controlled functions, except head of a product group

   See Chapter 2 Section 4.12 of your Study Text

15. **B** There is no requirement for the person whose information is being relied on to be approved nor to reside in the UK

   See Chapter 4 Section 2.6 of your Study Text

16. **C** The firm must withdraw any excess from the client money account the same day as it arises. For example, if a client repays a loan to the firm, these excess funds should be transferred the same day into the firm's own bank account. Conversely, if there were insufficient funds in the client money account, then the firm is required to make good the difference within the same time period

   See Chapter 4 Section 7.9 of your Study Text

17. **B** The maximum is two years in prison and an unlimited fine in a Crown Court

   See Chapter 4 Section 3.10 of your Study Text

18. **B** When the employee of the firm is not involved in making investment decisions regarding his/her portfolio that is discretionarily managed by a stockbroker, he or she does not need to report transactions on the portfolio to the firm

   See Chapter 4 Section 5.11 of your Study Text

19. **B** It is a Notice of Discontinuance that is issued where proceedings are no longer to be continued

   See Chapter 2 Section 2.1 of your Study Text

20.　C　A non-authorised firm may only communicate a financial promotion if an exemption applies under s21 of FSMA 2000 or it is approved by an authorised firm

See Chapter 4 Section 3 of your Study Text

21.　A　The financial crisis has brought calls for a move away from a 'light touch' regulatory regime

See Chapter 1 Section 6.3 of your Study Text

22.　D　DIEs do not conduct regulated activities in the UK and, therefore, do not need to be exempted from FSMA 2000. The designation is given by the FSA if they believe that the overseas exchange provides appropriate investor protections. Enterprise investment schemes, the IMF and RIEs are all exempt

See Chapter 2 Section 1.7 of your Study Text

23.　B　A review of appropriateness is a less onerous requirement on firms than that of suitability. A review of suitability is required whenever a firm makes a personal recommendation or manages investments. A review of appropriateness is required in other cases of investment services

See Chapter 4 Section 4 of your Study Text

24.　C　The requirement to state the research firm's holding in the subject or *vice versa* starts at 5%

See Chapter 4 Section 5.3.4 of your Study Text

25.　A　The requirement to execute a trade is to do so 'promptly' and there is no specific timeframe set out in COBS

See Chapter 4 Section 5.8 of your Study Text

26.　B　This is Threshold Condition 5 and the FSA could withdraw authorisation as a result of such a breach as the firm is no longer suitable to be authorised

See Chapter 2 Section 4.7 of your Study Text

27.　A　The FSA will not generally review the integrity of a major client of the applicant as part of the vetting process. However, the directors and partners of the applicant, any company in the same group as the applicant, or who controls the applicant, will be treated as being 'connected'

See Chapter 2 Section 4.8 of your Study Text

28.　D　A firm should have appropriate measures so it does **not** unreasonably deny access to its services to potential customers who find it difficult to show the usual type of evidence of identity, such as a utility bill in their own name

See Chapter 3 Section 3.7.1 of your Study Text

29.　D　Any spent convictions may be taken into account where relevant, but particular reference may be given to offences of dishonesty, fraud and financial crime

See Chapter 2 Section 4.10 of your Study Text

30.　B　As for many SYSC rules, this rule is mandatory for common platform firms but guidance for non-MiFID firms

See Chapter 1 Section 5.2 of your Study Text

31.   **C**   The Money Laundering Regulations require retention of records for five years

           See Chapter 3 Section 3.5 of your Study Text

32.   **C**   They may copy all relevant documents, but not remove them

           See Chapter 2 Section 3 of your Study Text

33.   **B**   These are the structured set of measures when a firm establishes a business relationship

           See Chapter 3 Section 3.10 of your Study Text

34.   **C**   The change must be publicised if the 3% threshold is crossed in either direction, and if full percentage points above 3% are crossed, again in either direction

           See Chapter 3 Section 5.3 of your Study Text

35.   **B**   The FSA's Handbook aims to be media-neutral, so that email and other forms of electronic communications are given the same status as paper communications. Exclusive use of a website for electronic communications requires the consent of the customer

           See Chapter 4 Section 1.4 of your Study Text

36.   **B**   Trade bills will not be considered as tradeable debt. They should not to be confused with Treasury Bills issued by the Debt Management Office which are tradeable and therefore would be classified as an investment

           See Chapter 2 Section 4.4 of your Study Text

37.   **B**   A firm or approved person who receives a Decision Notice or Supervisory Notice (including a third party who has been given a copy of the Decision Notice) has the right to appeal to the Upper Tribunal (Tax and Chancery Chamber)

           See Chapter 2 Section 2.6 of your Study Text

38.   **A**   A private warning is used by the FSA if it has cause for concern about the behaviour of an approved person, but believes it is not appropriate to carry out a disciplinary procedure. It is therefore not considered a 'formal' procedure

           See Chapter 2 Section 2.1 of your Study Text

39.   **B**   The role of the RDC is separate from that of the FSA supervision and enforcement teams in order to provide some level of independence in its decisions. Only the Chairman is an FSA employee

           See Chapter 2 Section 2.1 of your Study Text

40.   **C**   Property held directly by the investor is not a FSMA investment. However, buying units in a collective investment scheme that invests solely in property would be classed as a regulated activity under FSMA 2000

           See Chapter 2 Section 4.1 of your Study Text

41.   **C**   All of these are considered acts of misconduct and could be the subject of an FSA investigation with subsequent disciplinary action being imposed by the Regulatory Decisions Committee. The accused would then have the right to appeal within 28 days of the Decision Notice to the Upper Tribunal (Tax and Chancery Chamber)

           See Chapter 2 Section 2.7 of your Study Text

42.   **C**   Recognised Overseas Investment Exchanges get their recognition from the FSA

See Chapter 1 Section 7.5 of your Study Text

43.   **B**   In this scenario, the FSA will consider cancelling the firm's Part IV permission rather than varying its Part IV permission. In all of the other circumstances, the FSA may decide to vary the firm's Part IV permission

See Chapter 2 Section 4.6 of your Study Text

44.   **B**   Insider dealing legislation relates to the securities of companies (i.e. bonds and shares) and thus excludes foreign currencies. Debentures are a form of secured bonds

See Chapter 3 Section 1.1 of your Study Text

45.   **B**   The JMLSG Guidance Notes give firms an indication of best business practice in relation to money laundering systems and controls. As guidance notes, these are not compulsory. Nor can the JMLSG impose fines

See Chapter 3 Section 3.8.1 of your Study Text

46.   **B**   This is the same as the possible five years in jail for failure to report knowledge or suspicion of money laundering

See Chapter 3 Section 4.5 of your Study Text

47.   **D**   Be careful not to confuse the DPA requirements (which are drafted to cover all record keeping, and therefore use the general rule as no longer than is necessary) with the FSA rules

See Chapter 3 Section 6.2 of your Study Text

48.   **C**   The Final Notice confirms the information that was contained in the Decision Notice and which has either not been appealed or the appeal has failed

See Chapter 2 Section 2.1 of your Study Text

49.   **C**   Breach will have to be proven. Some principles will not apply to some firms performing certain regulated activities. Private persons have a right for action in damages when a breach of a rule has occurred

See Chapter 1 Section 2.1 to 2.5 of your Study Text

50.   **C**   Misleading Statements and Practices – S397 is a criminal offence. It is the insider dealing offence that concerns the use of unpublished information and applies only to individuals

See Chapter 2 Section 5 of your Study Text

Practice Examination 4

50 Questions in 1 Hour

1. **Information has come to light regarding an application for authorisation currently being considered by the FSA that may have an adverse effect on the applicant. The FSA will**

   A Proceed with the application ignoring the information as it has come to light after the application has been submitted

   B Proceed with the application taking account of the information depending on its validity and importance

   C Immediately halt the application and write to the applicant asking for a written response to the information that has come to light

   D Immediately stop the application and return all documentation to the applicant asking for a response to the information that has come to light

2. **Which statement regarding breaching FSA rules and enforcement is true?**

   A Warning Notices can be given orally

   B A further Decision Notice can only be sent within six months

   C There is a right of appeal after a Final Notice has been sent

   D A Decision Notice can differ in content from a further Decision Notice

3. **If a financial services firm that was not authorised enters into financial difficulties and is subsequently declared insolvent, what is the maximum compensation that could be received by a retail client who had paid £66,000 for investments with the firm under the Financial Services Compensation Scheme?**

   A £nil

   B £33,000

   C £50,000

   D £66,000

4. **On what basis can a firm deal before its research is published?**

   A Own account

   B Execution only

   C Discretionary client

   D Retail client

5. **Jack Jonson is retired and requests a copy Confirmation Notice of a deal with your firm seven years ago. You may tell him that**

    A Copies only have to be kept for six years

    B Copies may only be kept for up to five years

    C He should have applied within the year

    D He cannot have one because he is now retired

6. **Which of the following investments would not come under MiFID?**

    A Equity swaps

    B Derivatives

    C Commodities

    D Bonds

7. **Which one of these is not exempt from authorisation?**

    A London Stock Exchange

    B Lloyd's

    C Lloyd's members

    D Bank of England

8. **All of the following financial promotions would fall under the territorial scope of the FSA's Financial Promotions regulations, except**

    A A financial promotion made to an investor based in the UK

    B An unwritten cold call made to an investor based outside of the UK

    C Approving a financial promotion of an overseas person communicated at investors in the UK

    D A solicited unwritten financial promotion made to an overseas person

9. **Which one of the following are not permitted investments for a UCITS-compliant fund?**

    A Money market instruments

    B Commodity derivatives

    C Non-European equities

    D Investment grade bonds

10. **To which of the following will host state Conduct of Business rules apply?**

        I   A UK branch of an EEA passported investment firm

        II   Credit institution accepting deposits under MiFID

        III   EEA foreign exchange dealer passporting into UK

        IV   Appointed representative of an EEA investment firm

  A I and II

  B II and IV

  C II and III

  D I and IV

11. **Which of the following will not be classified as a *per se* eligible counterparty?**

  A International Monetary Fund

  B Commodity derivatives dealer

  C Large undertaking with share capital of £5m

  D Insurance company

12. **Which of the following is not a professional client?**

  A A company with 250 employees and balance sheet of €12.5 million

  B A company with called up share capital of £12 million

  C A large undertaking with €200,000 own funds and balance sheet of €20 million

  D Another FSA firm

13. **To which one of the following will COBS rules not apply?**

  A French investment adviser opening an office in the UK

  B UK firm opening a branch in an EEA member state

  C Appointed representative of an EEA firm providing services to UK investors

  D Cross border sales from EEA

14. **Suitability must be assessed**

  A For retail clients only

  B For retail clients always and professional clients at the discretion of the firm

  C For retail clients only in connection with personal recommendation

  D For retail clients always and professional clients at the discretion of the firm when providing a personal recommendation or managing client's investments

15. **The firm is not required to assess appropriateness when executing client orders in**

  A Units in a collective investment scheme

  B Derivatives

  C Warrants

  D Unlisted shares

16. **Conflicts of interests must be disclosed to the client**

    A   When it is reasonable to do so

    B   As a preventative measure

    C   When the conflict is unmanageable as a last resort only

    D   When providing independent investment research

17. **Which of the following is false regarding aggregation of orders?**

    A   It involves aggregating customer orders with other customers or with the firm's own orders

    B   Aggregation may only occur if there will never be a disadvantage to customers

    C   In partial allocations priority should generally be given to clients' orders over those of the firm

    D   The firm must disclose that aggregation may work to the disadvantage of the client

18. **Which of the following is true of the rule on inducements?**

    A   The rule only applies to retail clients

    B   Payments must be made by or on behalf of the client

    C   Third party payments are allowed if immaterial and disclosed in the conflicts of interest policy

    D   Third party payments are permitted if client consents

19. **Under MiFID, which is the responsibility of the host country?**

    A   Authorisation

    B   Fit and Proper test

    C   Suitability

    D   COBS

20. **Which of the following financial promotions can be approved by an authorised firm?**

    A   Web cam conference

    B   Newspaper advert

    C   Phone call

    D   Email correspondence

21. **Which of the following necessitates a basic written agreement for designated investment business?**

    A   Retail clients only

    B   Retail and professional clients only

    C   All clients

    D   Professional clients only

22. **If a client gives specific instructions for the execution of a trade, best execution may be waived**

   A   For that trade only

   B   For all subsequent trades until the client requests best execution again

   C   For that category of transactions only

   D   Best execution may not be waived

23. **Confirmations for regulated activities must be kept for**

   A   Three years from the date of trading

   B   Three years from the date of despatch

   C   Five years from the date of trading

   D   Five years from the date of despatch

24. **Which of the following is not the case when disclosing an interest?**

   A   The disclosure must be in writing

   B   The disclosure may be oral

   C   Disclosure must be made before undertaking discretionary transactions

   D   The disclosure can be communicated by electronic means

25. **When is it permissible to offer two execution venues where the firm applies different charges to clients?**

   A   It is not permissible in any circumstances

   B   It is only permissible if the two venues have different execution costs

   C   It is only permissible if these are the only two venues available

   D   It is only permissible if a professional client has given written consent

26. **Which of the following does not provide sufficient reason for a firm to rely on information provided by a third party?**

   A   The information is in provided in good faith

   B   The information is from a professional firm

   C   The information is from an EEA regulated firm and related to MiFID business

   D   The information is from a competent person

27. **If you receive a decision from the RDC, you are allowed to appeal to the Upper Tribunal (Tax and Chancery Chamber)**

   A   Within 28 days

   B   Within 60 days

   C   If the decision involved a fine of more than £10,000

   D   In no circumstances

28. **In a transaction, which is the most likely indication of terrorist activity rather than money laundering activity?**

    A   Funds coming from a legitimate source

    B   A very large transaction

    C   A trade representing an unusual pattern

    D   The trade is one of multiple transactions

29. **Which of the following is subject to the FSA's approved person regime?**

    A   Non-executive director

    B   Compliance assistant

    C   Product manager

    D   Human resources manager

30. **What is the maximum penalty for a firm conducting regulated activities when not authorised?**

    A   Six months imprisonment and/or a £5,000 fine

    B   Unlimited fine

    C   Two years imprisonment

    D   Two years imprisonment and an unlimited fine

31. **How would you categorise a company with €35m turnover, €18m balance sheet and €2.5m of own funds?**

    A   *Per se* professional client

    B   *Per se* counterparty

    C   Retail client

    D   Elective professional client

32. **Which of the following is false regarding a firm's conflicts policy?**

    A   It must be set out in writing

    B   It must be signed off by the FSA

    C   It needs to be appropriate to the size and organisation of the firm

    D   It needs to be appropriate to the nature, scale and complexity of its business

33. **What is the central purpose of FSA's principles-based regulatory approach?**

    A   To encourage firms to adopt a more ethical frame of mind

    B   To shift regulatory focus towards outcomes rather than compliance with detailed rules

    C   To limit the scope for fraud and abuse of power

    D   To ensure adequate protection for consumers

34.   **What can be used as a defence against S397 Misleading Statements and Practices?**

A   Market making

B   Stabilisation

C   Takeover rules

D   Market information

35.   **Which of the following is true of insider dealing and market abuse?**

A   Both may occur in relation to using unpublished information

B   Both apply to the same securities

C   The punishment for each is the same

D   Both are detailed in the Criminal Justice Act 1993

36.   **Who is most likely to be an insider?**

A   A person by virtue of their employment

B   Someone who has bought information

C   A person who has traded shares

D   Someone who has observed information

37.   **Who will always be protected from insider dealing when acting in good faith?**

A   A broker/dealer

B   A market maker

C   A fund manager

D   A person dealing for their own account

38.   **What is the main purpose of the UKLA's Model Code?**

A   To avoid suspicions of Directors engaging in insider dealing

B   To require Directors to keep investments for at least two years

C   To ensure that Directors do not issue shares to themselves without FSA approval

D   To prevent Directors selling short

39.   **Which of the following is true of a Multilateral Trading Facility (MTF)?**

A   It is a facility where a firm engages in multiple core investment schemes

B   It is a system where a firm provides services similar to those of exchanges by matching client orders

C   It is a system where a firm takes proprietary positions with a client

D   It is a facility where a firm operates in more than one location

40. **All of the following are possible defences against insider dealing, except**

   A The individual had not been trained by the employer

   B The individual would have done what he did even if he had not had the information

   C At the time, the individual believed on reasonable grounds that the information had been disclosed widely enough to ensure that none of those taking part in the dealing would be prejudiced by not having the information

   D The individual did not, at the time, expect the dealing to result in a profit

41. **Which of the following statements is false in relation to market abuse?**

   A It is contained in S118 FSMA

   B Standards expected by a regular market user will only be used in relation to the offences of a misuse of information, misleading behaviour and distortion

   C The market abuse regime is 'intent based' rather than 'effects based'

   D The maximum penalty is an unlimited fine

42. **Which of the following would be an example of breaching the Principle of Integrity, as it applies to approved persons?**

   A Failing to properly consider the business risk of a large expansion into a new area of business

   B Deliberately misleading a client over the nature of an investment

   C Not adequately disclosing the risks of a product

   D Delegating responsibility without ensuring that the person delegated to is suitable

43. **Details of financial sanctions imposed by the UK should be sought at the web site of**

   A Financial Services Authority

   B Department of Business, Innovation & Skills

   C Bank of England

   D HM Treasury

44. **How long does the FSA have to determine an application for authorisation from the date of receipt?**

   A 21 days

   B 28 days

   C Three months

   D Six months

   Approval – 3
   Authorisation – 6

45. **The Disclosure and Transparency Rules (DTR) do all of the following except**

   A Require issuers of securities to set up insider lists

   B Require companies to control access to inside information

   C Impose disclosure requirements in cases where there is suspicion of money laundering or terrorist financing

   D Impose notification requirements on shareholders of listed companies

46. **When may a firm make cold (unsolicited) calls?**

   A   From 08:30 to 20:30 Monday to Friday

   B   If the recipient has had an established client relationship with the firm such that the recipient envisages receiving them

   C   From 09:00 to 21:00 Monday to Saturday

   D   When the recipient has requested the call

47. **Which of the following statements about rules governing investment research activities is false?**

   A   Financial analysts can take positions in securities contrary to their current recommendations only in exceptional circumstances and with senior permission

   B   Analysts must refrain from dealing on the information contained in research until the clients have been provided with time to consider it

   C   Research analysts must not promise issuers favourable research coverage

   D   The issuer should be permitted to review unpublished research on their company at any time

48. **What should the authorised firm take reasonable steps to ensure is communicated in an oral financial promotion by its representative?**

   A   Firm is regulated by the Financial Services Authority

   B   Nature of the firm and its services

   C   Costs and charges

   D   Name of representative and of firm

49. **A Chairman is privy to price sensitive information. When can other directors deal in the company's shares?**

   A   If the Chairman provides express permission

   B   If the directors prove that they are not aware of the information

   C   If there is no restrictions on dealing in the close period

   D   If they are taking long positions rather than short positions

50. **Which of the following is a general defence against a charge of insider dealing?**

   A   Market maker acting in good faith

   B   A potential bidder buying a stake in a company

   C   Assumed that the information was widely known

   D   Acting under the rules of stabilisation

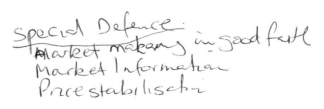

Answers

1. **C** It cannot be right for the FSA to continue processing the application without clarification of the issue that has come to light. Nor does it make sense to return all documentation since it will require it again once it has received clarification on the issue of concern

   See Chapter 2 Section 4.6 of your Study Text

2. **D** Logic dictates that a further notice would be different to a Decision Notice, otherwise why would it be sent? All the other statements are not true

   See Chapter 2 Section 2.1 of your Study Text

3. **A** If the firm which is insolvent was not an FSA-authorised firm, the investor is unable to seek compensation from the FSCS

   See Chapter 5 Section 3.2 of your Study Text

4. **B** Generally a firm cannot deal on behalf of other persons including the firm in relation to unpublished research until the recipients of the research have had a reasonable opportunity to act on it. The exceptions to this rule are the firm acting as a market maker in good faith and the firm executing an unsolicited client order

   See Chapter 4 Section 5.3 of your Study Text

5. **B** In relation to MiFID business, records of confirmations will need to be kept for at least five years. For non-MiFID business there is a three-year record keeping rule

   See Chapter 3 Section 6.4 of your Study Text

6. **C** The MiFID definition of a financial instrument is quite wide and will include for example transferable securities, money market instruments, units in a CIS and most type of derivatives. However, direct investment in commodities is not covered by MiFID

   See Chapter 3 Section 8.1.2 of your Study Text

7. **B** The LSE (a RIE), Lloyd's members and the Bank of England (one of the exempt institutions) are all exempt from authorisation. However, the Lloyd's market is authorised

   See Chapter 2 Section 1.7 of your Study Text

8. **D** As the overseas person has solicited the unwritten communication, the FSA rules do not apply. The rules do apply outside the UK in relation to financial promotions that are cold calls

   See Chapter 4 Section 3.9.3 of your Study Text

9. **B** Commodity derivatives are not covered by UCITS

   See Chapter 3 Section 8.2 of your Study Text

10. **D** Accepting deposits and stand-alone foreign exchange dealing are not covered by the MiFID definition of investment services and activities

    See Chapter 3 Section 8.1.2 of your Study Text

11. **C**   A large undertaking with share capital of £5m could be a *per se* professional client (for non-MiFID business) but not a *per se* eligible counterparty

See Chapter 4 Section 2.2.3 of your Study Text

12. **C**   The large undertaking in C would have to have at least €2m own funds and a balance sheet of at least €20m to be a professional client

See Chapter 4 Section 2.2 of your Study Text

13. **D**   Any cross-border sales follow home state rules. For other types of passported business, firms are generally required to follow host state COBS (so answers for A and C are not the correct answer) but there are exceptions to this, e.g. COBS rules on research and personal account dealing which follow home state COBS (therefore B is not the correct answer)

See Chapter 4 Sections 1.2 and 1.3 of your Study Text

14. **D**   In relation to MiFID business, the suitability rules apply to retail and professional clients. However, a firm is entitled to assume that for the products/services a professional client is correctly categorised as professional, it already has the necessary level of experience and knowledge

See Chapter 4 Section 4.1 of your Study Text

15. **A**   An appropriateness check is not required for certain non-complex financial instruments. Non-complex products include shares listed on a regulated market, money market instruments and units in a UCITS collective investment scheme. Complex products include warrants, derivatives and unlisted shares

See Chapter 4 Section 4.3.2 of your Study Text

16. **C**   Disclosure of a conflict should not be seen as a way of managing a conflict. Instead disclosure should be made where the conflict is unmanageable and as a last resort. Generally, conflicts are only disclosed in relation to non-independent research – not investment (independent) research

See Chapter 4 Section 5.2 of your Study Text

17. **B**   Aggregation is only permitted where it is unlikely to work to the disadvantage of any clients. Because the aggregation might disadvantage clients, this fact must be disclosed to clients before the aggregation takes place. For this reason, B is false

See Chapter 4 Section 5.9 of your Study Text

18. **C**   The rule on inducements applies to retail and professional clients. Inducements cover fees, commissions and non-monetary benefits paid to or by the client or someone on their behalf. Inducements are then only allowed if they do not impair compliance with the firm's duty to act in the best interests of the client and are generally disclosed in the conflicts of interest policy

See Chapter 4 Section 5.4 of your Study Text

19. **D**   Authorisation, fit and proper test and suitability (threshold conditions) are a Home State responsibility

See Chapter 4 Section 1.3 of your Study Text

20. **B** A firm approving a financial promotion must confirm that it complies with the financial promotions rules. Due to the interactive/live nature of a webcam conference, phone call and email correspondence, these types of promotion cannot be approved

See Chapter 4 Section 3.17 of your Study Text

21. **A** Firms carrying on designated investment business with retail clients (other than advising on investments) must give the client a basic written agreement

See Chapter 4 Section 2.5 of your Study Text

22. **A** When a firm executes an order following specific instructions from the client, it should be treated as having satisfied its best execution obligations only in respect of the part or aspect of the order to which the client instructions relate. The fact that the client has given specific instructions which cover one part or aspect of the order should not be treated as releasing the firm from its best execution obligations in respect of any other parts or aspects of the client order that are not covered by such instructions

See Chapter 4 Section 5.7.2 of your Study Text

23. **D** The general rule is that you should assume the question is referring to MiFID business unless it states otherwise. Copies of confirmation notes for MiFID business should be kept for five years from the date of despatch (three years for non-MiFID business)

See Chapter 3 Section 6.4 of your Study Text

24. **B** Where a firm's arrangements to manage conflicts of interest are not sufficient to ensure, with reasonable confidence, that risks of damage to the interests of a client will be prevented, the firm must clearly disclose the general nature and/or sources of conflicts of interest to the client before undertaking business for the client. The disclosure must be made in a durable medium and be sufficiently detailed to enable the client to take an informed decision in relation to the business to which the conflict of interest arises

See Chapter 4 Section 5.2 of your Study Text

25. **B** Where a firm has the ability to execute on more than one execution venue, it must take into account both its own costs and the costs of the relevant execution venue to establish which one would provide the best overall result. Commission structures must not discriminate between execution venues

See Chapter 4 Section 5.6 of your Study Text

26. **A** The COBS rule on reliance on others allows for information/instructions to be provided by MiFID firms, firms authorised in another EEA state and also information in writing from a competent person, e.g. an unconnected authorised person or a professional firm

See Chapter 4 Section 2.6 of your Study Text

27. **A** If you receive a decision from the RDC you have 28 days to refer to the Tribunal

See Chapter 2 Section 2.6 of your Study Text

28. **A** There are two main differences between money laundering funds and terrorist funds. These are that terrorist funds could come from a legitimate source and that terrorist financing usually involves much smaller amounts of money

See Chapter 3 Section 4.1 of your Study Text

29. **A**   A non-executive directorship is an example of a controlled function which requires approval by the FSA. Other examples include the functions of directors, chief executive, compliance officer and money laundering reporting officer, and the customer function

See Chapter 2 Section 4.12 of your Study Text

30. **D**   Two years in prison and an unlimited fine is the maximum penalty (in the Crown Court) for breaching s19 FSMA – called the general prohibition

See Chapter 2 Section 1.2 of your Study Text

31. **C**   A *per se* professional client must meet any two of the following criteria: balance sheet €20m, turnover €40m or own funds of €2m. This particular company only meets the own funds test and so must be categorised as a retail client

See Chapter 4 Section 2.2.3 of your Study Text

32. **B**   The FSA will not authorise or sign off any documentation relating to an authorised firm

See Chapter 4 Section 5.2 of your Study Text

33. **B**   A is the rationale behind the Treating Customers Fairly (TCF) initiative. D is one of the statutory regulatory objectives

See Chapter 1 Section 6.2 of your Study Text

34. **B**   Behaviour in accordance with the price stabilisation rules is a defence against a breach of s397 FSMA 2000

See Chapter 2 Section 5 of your Study Text

35. **A**   The market abuse provisions in s118 FSMA 2000 and the insider dealing legislation in the Criminal Justice Act 1993 contain offences relating to using unpublished information. Market abuse applies to qualifying investments traded on a prescribed market, whereas insider dealing relates to securities, debt and any related hybrid or derivative with trading taking place on a regulated market or through a professional intermediary. Penalties for market abuse include a fine whereas for insider dealing a jail term is possible

See Chapter 3 Sections 1 and 2 of your Study Text

36. **A**   Under the Criminal Justice Act 1993, an inside source includes those who receive information by virtue of their office or employment. Therefore A is the best available answer

See Chapter 3 Section 1.2 of your Study Text

37. **B**   A market maker acting in good faith is an example of one of the special defences in relation to insider dealing

See Chapter 3 Section 1.5.1 of your Study Text

38. **A**   Under the UKLA Model Code, directors are not able to trade during the close period. This is two months prior to the announcement of their half year or full year accounts. If directors cannot deal they are not going to be able to carry out insider dealing

See Chapter 3 Section 5.4 of your Study Text

39. **B**   A multilateral trading facility provides an alternative order matching system to an exchange. The client orders match with other clients so the firm operating the system does not take proprietary positions

See Chapter 1 Section 7.8 of your Study Text

40. **A**   Not being properly trained is a defence against failing to report certain money laundering suspicions, but it does not apply to insider dealing

See Chapter 3 Section 1.4 and 1.5 of your Study Text

41. **C**   The market abuse regime is 'effects-based' rather than 'intent-based'

See Chapter 3 Section 2.7 of your Study Text

42. **B**   Deliberate wrongdoing is an example of a breach of the Principle of Integrity

See Chapter 1 Section 2.3 of your Study Text

43. **D**   Responsibility for administration of financial sanctions in the UK transferred from the Bank of England to HM Treasury in October 2007

See Chapter 3 Section 4.8 of your Study Text

44. **D**   The FSA has six months to consider a firm's application for authorisation, but only three months to consider an application for approval for an employee performing a controlled function

See Chapter 2 Section 4.8 of your Study Text

45. **C**   DTR covers A, B and D, but not anti-money laundering disclosures

See Chapter 3 Section 5.1 to 5.3 of your Study Text

46. **B**   The recipient requesting a call cannot be described as a 'cold call' because the call was requested. There are no specified time limits in COBS for when cold calls may be made

See Chapter 5 Section 3.15 of your Study Text

47. **D**   Pre-publication drafts can be previewed by the issuer only for the purpose of verifying compliance

See Chapter 4 Section 5.3 of your Study Text

48. **D**   The suitability rule applies where firms make personal recommendations relating to designated investments and where firms manage investments. Therefore D is the best available answer

See Chapter 4 Section 4.1 of your Study Text

49. **A**   Directors must seek permission from the Chairman of the company before they are able to buy or sell shares in the company

See Chapter 3 Section 5.4 of your Study Text

50. C   This question requires you to know the difference between the general defences and special defences. The three special defences are market making in good faith, market information and acting in accordance with the price stabilisation rules. Believing on reasonable grounds that the information is widely known is an example of a general defence

See Chapter 3 Sections 1.4 and 1.5 of your Study Text

Practice Examination 5

50 Questions in 1 Hour

1.   **With respect to the disciplinary process, which of these statements is true?**

A   The action announced in the Decision Notice can be different from that proposed in the Warning Notice

B   The FSA must issue a Final Notice within six months of issuing a Decision Notice

C   The FSA may issue a Final Notice in place of a Decision Notice

D   There is no right of appeal to a Further Decision Notice

2.   **Which of the following might the FSA accept as a defence against market abuse?**

A   The person did not believe that they were committing an offence

B   The person is an approved person

C   The person is not performing an approved function

D   The person is a regular user

3.   **An IFA approaches an investment firm to execute a transaction on behalf of a client. Which of the following is true?**

A   The IFA is responsible for the accuracy of transaction information

B   The investment firm must check that client information is correct

C   The IFA is responsible for checking that the product is suitable and the investment firm is responsible for checking appropriateness

D   The investment firm must provide the underlying client with a client agreement

4.   **Which of these meets the requirement for a firm to treat an undertaking as a professional client for MiFID business?**

A   Net turnover of €40,000,000

B   Own funds of €1,000,000 and net assets of €40,000,000

C   Own funds of €2,000,000 and balance sheet total of €25,000,000

D   Balance sheet total of €20,000,000

5.   **Which of the following is not a MiFID investment?**

A   Warrant

B   Physical commodity

C   Gold future

D   High coupon corporate bond

6. **A disgruntled former Director of ABC plc makes a false statement on an internet chat site about ABC plc with the intention on launching a bear raid. Under what provisions could he face criminal charges?**

    A   Criminal Justice Act 1993

    B   Financial Services and Markets Act 2000

    C   Money Laundering Regulations 2007

    D   Public Interest Disclosure Act 1998

7. **Which of these is most likely to be an insider?**

    A   An employee working in the finance department of XYZ

    B   A person who observed information on XYZ

    C   A shareholder in XYZ who sold some shares after the announcement of a profits warning

    D   An investor who bought shares in XYZ after they were recommended to him by his broker

8. **Which of these potentially has a general defence to insider dealing?**

    A   A market maker acting in good faith

    B   A broker appointed to stabilise a new issue

    C   An investor who is building his stake in preparation for launching a takeover bid

    D   An investor who bought shares based on information that he believed was generally available

9. **Who will prosecute market abuse offences?**

    A   FSA

    B   HM Treasury

    C   Upper Tribunal (Tax and Chancery Chamber)

    D   SOCA

10. **With respect to the Data Protection Act, which of the following is true?**

    A   Data cannot be transferred outside of the European Economic Area

    B   If information has been legally collected it can then be used in any way that the controller sees fit

    C   Information must be accurate and up to date

    D   Information can be kept indefinitely

11. **Which type of notice can only be issued with the consent of the recipient?**

    A   Warning Notice

    B   Notice of Discontinuance

    C   Decision Notice

    D   Further Decision Notice

12. **Which of the following would not be classified as a specified investment?**

    A   Forward rate agreement

    B   Interest rate swap

    C   Collective investment scheme

    D   NS&I Savings Certificates

13. **A fund manager wants to market his fund under the provisions of UCITS III. Which is he not allowed to invest in?**

    A   Money market instruments

    B   High dividend yield equities

    C   Platinum

    D   Shares in a split capital investment trust

14. **Which of the following is true regarding the rule on inducements?**

    A   It is designed to prohibit the firm making payments to a third party for investment services

    B   It requires firms to put a monetary value on the client entertaining that it benefits from

    C   The client must sign to indicate that they are aware of the potential conflicts of interest arising from inducements

    D   It prevents firms from accepting payments that may act counter to the best interest of their clients

15. **The FSA issues a Warning Notice to an individual. Which of the following could happen next?**

    A   The FSA will issue a Decision Notice

    B   The FSA will publish the Warning Notice to the public

    C   The individual can apply to the Upper Tribunal (Tax and Chancery Chamber)

    D   The individual may enter into discussion to settle with the FSA

16. **Which of these is the best description of one of the statutory objectives of the FSA?**

    A   To promote orderly and efficient markets

    B   To enforce punishments against money laundering

    C   To ensure that all EU Directives are brought into UK rules

    D   To ensure that all individuals working in financial services are approved

17. **All of the following Statements of Principle apply only to controlled functions with significant influence, except which one?**

    A   Must comply with all of the regulatory requirements

    B   Due skill, care and diligence in management

    C   Observe proper standards of market conduct

    D   Business of the firm is organised and controlled effectively

18. **Which of the following statements is true regarding the CISI (formerly SII) Code of Conduct?**

A It applies only when there are no other rules or guidance

B It is obligatory that all members follow the Code with the exception of when conducting business with eligible counterparties

C It is obligatory that all members follow the Code at all times

D It is guidance only and is not obligatory

19. **You are appointed as your firm's Data Protection Officer. With whom should you register?**

A The Serious Organised Crime Agency

B The Ministry of Information

C The Information Commissioner

D The Financial Services Authority

20. **Which of the following would be classified as undertaking designated investment business?**

A A trustee of a charitable trust

B The operator of an employee share scheme

C A family member overseeing the state of a deceased person

D The operator of a stakeholder pension scheme

21. **What is a possible outcome of entering into a contract to provide financial services when the activity is regulated but the firm has not been authorised by the FSA?**

A Contracts entered in to will be void

B Contracts entered into cannot be enforced on the client

C Contracts can be declared void by the Magistrate's Court

D Contracts can be declared void by the FSA

22. **If, after formal proceedings, the FSA determines that a disciplinary offence has occurred, which of the following will the FSA not do?**

A Issue a private censure

B Issue a public censure

C Impose a restitution order

D Issue a fine

23. **Mr Pink provides detailed internal information about the company he works for to Mr Blue. The company is a market leader in the building of reservoirs. Mr Pink informs Mr Blue that the information is not public, is price-sensitive and tells Mr Blue that he should not trade based on this information. Mr Blue ignores his advice and buys shares in the company. He makes a significant profit when the information is later released to the market. Who is guilty of insider trading according to the rules on market abuse?**

   A   Mr Pink only

   B   Mr Blue only

   C   Neither Mr Pink nor Mr Blue

   D   Both Mr Pink and Mr Blue

24. **Which of the following would be an insider according to the Criminal Justice Act 1993?**

   A   A director of a company who acts as a broker for that company's shares

   B   An employee of a company who buys shares following a purchase of shares by a non-executive director

   C   A junior on the audit team who sells shares based on his exposure to information in the unpublished company accounts

   D   An employee who sells shares as a result of a market rumour that the company is about to release a profit warning

25. **The close period before publication of the half-yearly report (in which directors must not deal in shares of their company) ends with publication of the report and begins**

   A   Two weeks before publication

   B   One month before publication

   C   Two months before publication

   D   At the end of the half year reported on

26. **With what sort of clients would a firm have to check that they understand the nature and risks of products being recommended under an advisory agreement?**

   A   Retail clients only

   B   Retail and professional clients only

   C   All clients

   D   Eligible counterparties only

27. **Which of the following deals or trades would not be an exception to the rules on personal account dealing?**

   A   Buying shares on behalf of your wife/husband

   B   Buying life assurance

   C   Your discretionary fund manager purchasing shares

   D   Buying units in an index tracking exchange traded fund

28. **What is the required delay before trading under the rules on dealing ahead of research?**

    A   The firm must wait until the market price has responded

    B   The firm must allow a reasonable time for the clients to react before placing its own trades

    C   One working day

    D   There is no required delay once the information is public

29. **Which one of the following will be subject to the FSA's approved person's regime?**

    A   A line manager in an authorised firm

    B   An employee responsible for client liaison

    C   An employee of an authorised firm responsible for training

    D   An employee who provides advice to customers of the firm

30. **Which of the following would be deemed to be client money?**

    A   A remittance, part of which is to pay the fees of the firm

    B   A deposit accepted by a bank

    C   Funds received to settle a transaction with a Unit Trust manager

    D   Funds held in a client account above the client money requirement

31. **Which of the following can be deemed to be eligible for compensation under the Financial Services Compensation Scheme?**

    A   A Government Department

    B   A collective investment scheme with net assets of £600m

    C   A manufacturing company whose annual turnover is £700,000

    D   An charitable trust with assets of £2.8 million

32. **A firm, ABC, is handling the potential merger of company X with company Y. This is not public information. A retail customer calls and asks ABC to execute a sell order on company X. What should ABC do?**

    A   Execute the order as requested

    B   Execute the order but disclose the conflict of interest

    C   Agree to execute the order but delay the trade until the merger is announced to allow the client to benefit from the expected rise in share price

    D   Decline to act due to the unmanageable conflict of interest

33. **A Treasury direction to financial sector firms under the Counter-Terrorism Act 2008 may not relate to**

    A   Ceasing business

    B   Limiting business

    C   Reporting

    D   An EEA country

34. **Gabriel is an account administrator for a bank. He has been opening accounts and accepting a lot of funds in cash from a director of a small overseas company. Which of the following stages of money laundering might he have been participating in?**

   A Layering

   B Integration

   C Settlement

   D Placement

   Placement | layering | Integration

35. **Which of the following is true regarding the FSA's rules on client assets?**

   A The firm can use funds held for a client in the course of their business activities

   B Funds held for a client should be segregated from funds of the firm

   C The client will always rank as a general creditor of the firm

   D Funds held for eligible counterparties are never treated as client assets

36. **The systems and controls function must involve reporting to the governing body of a firm on all of the following matters except which one?**

   A Setting and control of the firm's risk exposure

   B The firm's financial affairs

   C The firm's performance on Treating Customers Fairly

   D Adherence to internal procedures

37. **An employee, who acts as a discretionary manager for a retail client, executes an order with her own money. How can she best ensure compliance with her firm's procedures with regards to this trade?**

   A Gain permission from the firm and hold the investment for longer than a month

   B Gain permission from the firm and notify the firm that the trade has taken place

   C Check for any conflicts of interest, and if one is identified, cancel the trade

   D Notify the firm and execute the trade through a firm account

38. **Which of the following is true when a firm is providing discretionary management services to a retail client?**

   A A client agreement can be sent out after beginning the provision of services if the client requests this

   B If the client is based overseas, there is no need to send out a client agreement

   C A client agreement does not need to be sent if the client consents to this

   D A client agreement needs to be sent out before engaging in designated business activity

39. **Which of the following is true with respect to the FSA's rules on aggregation of orders?**

   A The client need not give consent to aggregation

   B The firm must disclose to the customer any disadvantages that aggregation may cause

   C The costs of the trade must be reduced

   D The firm can not aggregate customer orders with firm orders

40. **To which one of the following is the FSA's statutory power to request information limited?**

   A Only specific information can be requested

   B There are no limits to the type of information that can be requested

   C The information will have to be requested in the course of a meeting where legal counsels of the firm are present

   D The information will have to be requested in writing

41. **A company's Chairman is aware of price-sensitive information about his company of which all other directors are unaware. A director approaches him asking permission to deal in the company's shares. Which of the following is the correct way this should be handled?**

   A The director would be permitted to deal only once the information that the Chairman is aware of gets announced to the market

   B The director would be allowed to deal with the Chairman's permission

   C The director would not be permitted to deal

   D The Chairman would assign responsibility to the CEO to make the decision because of his difficult position

42. **Which types of clients require a written agreement for non-MiFID business?**

   A Private clients

   B Retail clients

   C All customers

   D All discretionary and advisory customers

43. **Which of the following do not require to be approved before use?**

   A A telephone communication

   B A website promotion

   C A radio advertisement

   D A promotion communicated in a national newspaper

44. **Where a firm identifies an unavoidable conflict that could damage the client's interests, what action must it take?**

   A Tell the client that they are unable to do business

   B Disclose the conflict to the client and let the client decide how to proceed

   C Tell the client and then proceed on the basis that a warning has been issued

   D Contact the FSA to seek advice

45. **When executing a firm's own account trade and a client trade, which of the following applies?**

    A The firm order must be executed first if it is likely to improve the terms of a deal for the client

    B The order of precedence is determined by the volume of the trade

    C The client order should always be executed first

    D Orders should normally be executed sequentially

46. **How often should an authorised firm submit a complaints summary report to the FSA?**

    A Monthly

    B Quarterly

    C Twice a year

    D Annually

47. **A firm has applied for approval on behalf of one of its employees. When will they be able to perform a controlled function?**

    A Once the application has been received by the FSA

    B When the FSA has provided written confirmation of approval

    C The employee can immediately begin performing the control function under supervision, until approval is granted or refused

    D The employee has a six-week grace period during which his activities will be supervised

48. **Which of the below is not one of the 'Statements of Principle'?**

    A Proper standard of market conduct

    B Integrity when performing a controlled function

    C Skill, care and diligence in performing a controlled function

    D Skill and care in safeguarding client assets

49. **Which of the following is an example of money laundering?**

    A A number of transactions designed to cover up the source of money

    B Passing on price sensitive information that leads to dealing

    C Using the media to disseminate false rumours about a company

    D A wash transaction

50. **Under the Terrorism Act 2000, when specifically should you report a suspicion?**

    A As soon as is reasonably practicable

    B By the next business day

    C By the end of the week

    D Without delay

Answers

1. **A**   After listening to anything that the accused has to say in mitigation, the RDC is at liberty to amend the Warning Notice when they issue the Decision Notice

     See Chapter 2 Section 2.1 of your Study Text

2. **A**   It is a possible defence that, on reasonable grounds, the person believed that the behaviour in question did not amount to market abuse

     See Chapter 3 Section 2.11 of your Study Text

3. **A**   As an authorised person, the IFA has responsibility for assessing the suitability of a transaction on which a personal recommendation is based. The investment firm does not have a responsibility to the underlying client

     See Chapter 4 Section 4.1 of your Study Text

4. **C**   You need to learn the criteria since the examiner may test these facts

     See Chapter 4 Section 2.2.3 of your Study Text

5. **B**   Physical commodities such as oil, gold and wheat are not MiFID investments. Derivatives on commodities are MiFID investments

     See Chapter 3 Section 8.1.2 of your Study Text

6. **B**   This is a breach of s397 which is an offence under FSMA 2000

     See Chapter 2 Section 5 of your Study Text

7. **A**   From the choices available, the best answer is 'an employee'. The other scenarios just describe market participants performing regular activities

     See Chapter 3 Section 1.2 of your Study Text

8. **D**   The other answers describe special defences

     See Chapter 3 Section 1.4 and 1.5 of your Study Text

9. **A**   It is the FSA who will seek to prosecute for market abuse offences

     See Chapter 3 Section 2.1 of your Study Text

10. **C**   One of the principles of the Data Protection Act 1998 is that information must be accurate and up-to-date

     See Chapter 3 Section 6 of your Study Text

11. **D**   A Further Decision Notice can only be sent once the recipient has received a Decision Notice and has exercised his/her right to appeal to the Upper Tribunal (Tax and Chancery Chamber)

     See Chapter 2 Section 2.3 of your Study Text

12. **D**   Products offered by National Savings & Investments (NS&I) are not specified investments

     See Chapter 2 Section 4.4 of your Study Text

13. **C** Physical commodities are not permitted as an investment vehicle

    See Chapter 3 Section 8.1.2 of your Study Text

14. **D** The intention of the inducements rule is to protect the best interests of a firm's clients

    See Chapter 4 Section 5.4 of your Study Text

15. **A** Warning Notices are not published to the public. Individuals only apply to the Upper Tribunal (Tax and Chancery Chamber) after the issuance of a Decision Notice. Individuals can enter into discussions to settle with the FSA but this would be before the RDC gets involved

    See Chapter 2 Section 2.1 of your Study Text

16. **A** A key objective of the FSA is to maintain market confidence

    See Chapter 1 Section 1.3 of your Study Text

17. **C** This question is asking which of the Statements of Principle apply to all types of controlled functions. Remember that significant influence functions are those controlled functions that also have senior management responsibilities

    See Chapter 1 Section 3.2 of your Study Text

18. **C** The CISI's Code of Conduct should always be observed

    See Chapter 1 Section 4.2 of your Study Text

19. **C** You are required to register with the Information Commissioner

    See Chapter 3 Section 6.1 of your Study Text

20. **D** The other activities are excluded

    See Chapter 2 Section 4.3 of your Study Text

21. **B** This is the best available answer. The customer is in a powerful position in that he/she can enforce the contract if it is in his/her favour or can insist that it is voided

    See Chapter 2 Section 4.6 of your Study Text

22. **A** A private censure is used for less serious offences

    See Chapter 2 Sections 2.5 and 2.7 of your Study Text

23. **D** Here Mr Pink has passed on information when he should not have and Mr Blue has acted on this information. Given that market abuse is 'effects based', both parties are guilty

    See Chapter 3 Section 2 of your Study Text

24. **C** Strictly it could be argued that all are inside sources but, given that the junior on the audit team acted on unpublished information, this is the best answer

    See Chapter 3 Section 1.2 of your Study Text

25. **D** This is to avoid any suspicions of improper dealing

    See Chapter 3 Section 5.4 of your Study Text

26. **A** Although there is a need to ensure that a trade is suitable with respect to a professional client's objectives and financial situation, knowledge and experience can be assumed

See Chapter 4 Section 4.1 of your Study Text

27. **A** The rule on personal account dealing is designed to prevent people taking advantage of privileged information. Buying into a life policy or investing in a collective investment scheme would not be a concern since it does not involve direct investment in the company of whom one has the privileged information. There is also an exclusion if it is a fund manager, not the person holding the information, who makes the purchase. This is on the assumption that there has been no communication between the two parties

See Chapter 4 Section 5.11 of your Study Text

28. **B** COBS is worded such that firms must provide clients with a 'reasonable opportunity to act'

See Chapter 4 Section 5.3.2 of your Study Text

29. **D** An employee would have to be advising customers (retail or professional) in order to be required to gain approved status for the customer function

See Chapter 2 Section 4.10 and 4.11 of your Study Text

30. **A** The fees payable to the firm are not classified as client money but the balance would be

See Chapter 4 Section 7 of your Study Text

31. **C** An enterprise with annual turnover of less than €2million (a 'micro-enterprise') is an eligible claimant

See Chapter 5 Section 1.2 of your Study Text

32. **A** The firm should execute the trade since it is an unsolicited trade. The consequence of avoiding the trade might be to alert suspicions in the client that an announcement is forthcoming. Normally Chinese wall arrangements should prevent those dealing with the order from knowing about the firm handling the potential merger

See Chapter 4 Section 5.2.4 of your Study Text

33. **D** A Treasury direction under the Act must relate to a non-EEA country. It may relate to customer due diligence, ongoing monitoring, systematic reporting and to limiting or ceasing business

See Chapter 3 Section 4.9 of your Study Text

34. **D** Remember the stages of money laundering: placement, layering and integration

See Chapter 3 Section 3.2 of your Study Text

35. **B** The basic idea of the client money rules is that client money and firm money should be kept separate

See Chapter 4 Section 7 of your Study Text

36. **C** TCF is not one of the specific headings to be reported on under this controlled function

See Chapter 2 Section 4.11 of your Study Text

37. **B**   The key here is that she should gain permission before trading

See Chapter 4 Section 5.11 of your Study Text

38. **A**   This is allowed if the transaction is agreed at a distance (e.g. telephone)

See Chapter 4 Section 2.5 of your Study Text

39. **B**   Whilst it is expected that benefits will be gained through aggregation, this is by no means certain. Thus, there is a requirement to explain this to clients

See Chapter 4 Section 5.9 of your Study Text

40. **D**   The power to request information is given by s165 of FSMA 2000, FSA can request any information but the request will need to be in writing

See Chapter 2 Section 3 of your Study Text

41. **B**   The fact that the Chairman is aware of price-sensitive information does not preclude other directors from trading

See Chapter 3 Section 1 of your Study Text

42. **B**   In this case, a written agreement is only required for retail clients

See Chapter 4 Section 2.5 of your Study Text

43. **A**   Since a telephone call is a real-time communication, it is not possible to approve it beforehand

See Chapter 4 Section 3.17 of your Study Text

44. **B**   Before undertaking business, the firm should disclose the conflict of interest to the client in sufficient detail for the client to make an informed decision

See Chapter 4 Section 5.2.2 of your Study Text

45. **D**   A firm will not be reprimanded for dealing on a 'time-stamp' basis. However, they are able to use their market knowledge to deal outside time-stamp order if this is likely to benefit one client without adversely affecting another client

See Chapter 4 Section 5.8 of your Study Text

46. **C**   Firms must log complaints and report twice a year, even if no complaints are received

See Chapter 5 Section 1.11 of your Study Text

47. **B**   Individuals can only perform a controlled function after they have been granted approved person status by the FSA

See Chapter 2 Section 4.12 of your Study Text

48. **D**   Whilst there is a requirement to responsibly safeguard client assets, this is not a Statement of Principle for Approved Persons

See Chapter 1 Section 3.2 of your Study Text

49.   A   This describes the layering process. The other scenarios describe insider dealing and s397 FSMA offences

See Chapter 3 Section 3.2 of your Study Text

50.   A   The requirement is to report 'as soon as is reasonably practicable'. The examiner does sometimes pick up on the actual wording that is used

See Chapter 3 Section 4.5 of your Study Text